Seeking the Silent Stranger

Seeking the Silent Stranger

Drawing Your Way into the Deeper Self

LIDIA E. EVERETT, M.D.

and

HYACINTHE KULLER BARON

Commune-A-Key Publishing
Salt Lake City

This book is designed as a tool to assist the reader to access their creativity. If you are currently being treated for an emotional or psychological disorder, or if your personal history suggests that you may need psychotherapeutic assistance, the authors recommend that you seek professional guidance before, during and after reading this book. If the reader experiences undesirable results, consequences or behaviors, the authors and publisher are not to be held responsible.

Everett, Lidia, E.
    Seeking the silent stranger: drawing your way into the deeper self / by Lidia E. Everett, M.D. and Hyacinthe Kuller Baron.
        p.   cm.
    Includes bibliographical references and index.
    ISBN: 1881394-02-6 (alk. paper)
    I. Creation (Literary, artistic, etc.) 2. Self-actualization (Psychology)—Problems, exercises, etc. 3. Art—Psychology.
    4. Charcoal drawing—Technique. I. Baron, Hyacinthe Kuller.
    II. Title.
    BF411.E94 1998
    153.3—dc21   97-48968
                                                                          CIP

Editorial: Caryn Summers and Nancy Lang
Cover design: Lightbourne Images, Ashland, Oregon
Cover drawing: Hyacinthe Kuller Baron
Interior design & typesetting: Connie Disney

$14.95 USA
$20.95 CANADA

To my citadel,
Sofia Agusta Antunez de Ramirez,
and my loving family.

—LIDIA

To my beloved Ed,
the Black Stallion, my knight in shining armor
who slays all the dragons in my life and to my Price Valiant,
my son the poet, Christopher Baron.

—HYACINTHE

TABLE OF CONTENTS

LIST OF ILLUSTRATIONS

"When I was a child, I spoke like a child,
I thought like a child, I reasoned like a child. When I became an adult,
I put an end to childish things."

—Corinthians 13:11

ACKNOWLEDGMENTS

I AM GREATLY INDEBTED to the following for their advice and support: our editor and publisher, Caryn Summers who shared the vision, edited the excesses, clarified my thoughts and inspired me with her enthusiasm; my husband John for his understanding and patience during this project; our subjects who, by their participation, helped to articulate the postulates that led to the definition of the *Silent Stranger*; the "Search" group of Santa Maria and Father Gerald who illuminated my path and gave me the spiritual fortitude to persevere; Dean Shannon for managing my family while I was bound to my computer; Lilia, who believed in me; and all of my dear friends who still recognized me and remembered my name when this project was finished.

Lidia E. Everett, M.D.
August 1997
San Diego, California

❖ ❖ ❖

THIS BOOK WAS INSPIRED by my students whose efforts helped me to refine the *Making Your Mark*™ technique and exercises and by their participation in *MYM*™ workshops at the San Diego Center for the Blind. They helped define the *Silent Stranger* as the adult creator of inner visions.

ACKNOWLEDGMENTS

Thank you to my mentors for recognizing talent and to all my collectors who made it possible for a woman to pursue an artistic career for more than forty years.

To my husband Ed, for his contribution and support. He made it possible for me to live and work in the garden of creativity and inspired the passion flower. To my son Steven, for life's lessons learned. To my son Christopher, whose own genius has validated creativity.

Finally, thank you to Caryn Summers, our editor, whose own search provided valuable recognition and input that made this book a reality.

My appreciation to "The Mother" for life's sacred blessings and profound connections.

Hyacinthe Kuller Baron
August, 1997
San Diego, California

A Portrait of the Silent Stranger

The nidus of our being.

The core of our esthetic aspirations.

The expressive culmination of our creativity.

An artist.

An artistic individual.

The creator of impressions.

The source of our inspiration

The protector of our emotional reactions.

The perceiver of our internal and external
stimulations.

A master storyteller who creates our unique
mythology through imagery.

—Hyacinthe's impression of
the Silent Stranger (Illustration #2)

Symbiosis
(Illustration #2)

INTRODUCTION

THE PHYSICIAN WANTED to learn to draw toucans. The artist was willing to teach her a technique that involved rubbing charcoal-soiled fingers on paper. During the lesson, the physician was preoccupied with the silliness of the situation. Charcoal soot was everywhere and the desired toucan did not materialize. Contrariwise, there was a disruptive internal voice that chastised the physician throughout the experience. What eventually did emerge was a totally unexpected drawing. Based on this drawing, the physician and the artist eventually decided to investigate the significance of the internal voice and how it affected creativity.

The physician felt she had bypassed a block when she ignored the mocking inner voice and did the technique anyway. She felt her rendition was about things she hadn't considered since she was a youngster. The artist disclaimed even owning an inner voice: she just wanted to teach people to draw. Together, they approached the mystery with the physician observing (science), and the artist teaching (art), until they found a common thread: every subsequent student they taught, observed and questioned said there was a part of themselves they were no longer in contact with, a stranger within them all. When they soiled their hands with charcoal grit and stroked their impressions on paper, they were sensing and seeing from a different perspective. They felt closer to the strangeness within themselves. As the students progressed in the exercises and learned to ignore their inner critical voice, they developed a capacity to see images totally out of context with their original intent.

They had met their "Silent Stranger."[1] This "Stranger" introduced itself by revealing hidden images in the smears they were utilizing to express themselves.

The "Silent Stranger" became known to them as their "Adult Creator."[2]

This book is not meant to be didactic nor dictatorial. The theory upon which it was written was investigated analytically by applying the techniques to thirty subjects. Each subject was asked to complete fourteen drawing exercises. Their reactions were elicited by asking questions or recording their responses as they spontaneously occurred. After several days the subjects were asked to review their drawings and any further input was recorded. Creative dialogue or personal stories were used to emphasize a point or to allow the reader to participate in a subject's revelations as they experienced techniques utilized in the exercises. The authors' wishes were to guide the reader through their search for the "Silent Stranger" so that they could become mutual participants in the search.

In this book, the authors share a part of the dialogue and adventures they encountered as they wandered through and into the world of the "Silent Stranger." There were countless playful moments and many intense arguments—until the authors realized that Lidia's science and Hyacinthe's art—while using different terminology, were expressing the same concepts. Furthermore, they discovered that each discipline could learn from the other. The authors concluded

---

1. The "Silent Stranger" is the pristine, creative spirit that communicates visually with us. It is neither an inner-child nor a socialized adult, but a melding of both. Its role in the creative process is as the "Adult Creator."

2. The "Adult Creator" is the "Silent Stranger's" role in the creative process.

that the time had come for science to soften its lofty definitions, and for art to define its vague conquests.

We have used charcoal and the tactile senses to stimulate imagery. Once you understand the "Stranger's" method of communication, you will be able to develop your own method of accessing the "Stranger's" creative gifts.

Reading this book and utilizing the creative exercises within it will introduce you to your own "Silent Stranger." The tools you will be given are not meant to relieve you of life's many ills, but to empower you to confront and change them.

You will find the adult creator within that will help you be as original as you desire and as your lifestyle choices permit!

You will set new and adventurous goals for yourself!

You will find inner-peace mediated by the spiritual high of self-discovery!

When you have finished reading this book, you will not go back to the loneliness of missing the stranger within you. In completing the exercises, you will have made your unique mark and bridged the mysterious chasm between faith and knowledge!

The Authors
San Diego, California
August 1997

Seeking the Silent Stranger

CHAPTER ONE

≈

The Discovery

A mysterious drawing done during an art lesson inspired the authors to investigate its derivation. A critical inner-voice seemed to block the execution of the drawing. Was the removal of this voice a key to unlocking self-expression and creativity?

Your hearts know in silence the secrets of the days and the nights.
But your ears thirst for the sound of your heart's knowledge.
You would know in words that which you have always known in
thought.
You would touch with your fingers the naked body of your dreams.

And it is well you should.

The hidden well-spring of your soul must needs rise and run
murmuring to the sea;
And the treasure of your infinite depths would be revealed to your eyes.
But let there be no scales to weigh your unknown treasure;
And seek not the depths of your knowledge with staff or sounding line.
For self is a sea boundless and measureless.
Say not, "I have found the truth," but rather, "I have found a truth."
Say not, "I have found the path of the soul."
Say rather, "I have met the soul walking upon my path."
For the soul walks upon all paths.
The soul walks not upon a line, neither does it grow like a reed.
The soul unfolds itself, like a lotus of countless petals.

—KAHLIL GIBRAN

Lidia: San Diego, California, 1997

The day started the same as any sunny morning at the marina except that a new tenant had moved in: an ancient, plastic-wrapped boat. It was suspended, prevented from sinking into the depths of the bay, by its tattered mooring lines. Perched, in similar disarray, on the back deck in a rococo chair was a white-haired gentlewoman with the most mischievous countenance I had ever seen. She cackled at my passing, so I turned back to introduce myself.

Hyacinthe was one of those 'artsy' types. She would begin and end most conversations with some bizarre explanation of the whys and wherefores of life's deeper meanings. She was intent on understanding and explaining every nuance of existence. She plucked wisps of ideas out of the air and wove them into a gossamer network of possibilities. The possibilities were often improbabilities, and it would have been easy to poke holes in her philosophies, but it was pleasant and fun to find myself in her fascinating flights of fantasy.

The content of our conversations bordered on crazed and scattered. Any passer-by would assume a free-association session was underway. As Hyacinthe bemoaned the alienation of mankind, I reasoned with her that things could be worse, that we could have all been born sociopaths.

Hyacinthe didn't tolerate my intellectualizing for long. I didn't tolerate her flight of ideas. Then she challenged me to draw, to make my mark. I accepted the challenge and found myself sitting in her studio rubbing charcoal all over my fingertips.

"Draw water," said Hyacinthe to her reluctant student. "Close your eyes and feel the water. Stroke your feelings about water onto the paper with your fingertips." My internal dialogue spoke: *"What does this have to do with any concept of drawing? She wants water, fine!... Gee, this is dirty business. I've got filthy charcoal all over the place... Hmmm... Is this what water feels like?... Well, let's just stroke away and get this over with."*

"Lidia, that's absolutely fabulous! You really captured the essence of the water. Now try to make your impression of this coffee mug. Don't use lines, just imagine where the light is coming from and use your fingers," Hyacinthe commanded as she plopped a silly, stained coffee mug on the table.

I squinted at her and judged her to be dictatorial, parental and absurd. How would I know where the light was coming from? I'm no artist and she certainly wasn't helping me to become one.

I stroked out the cup.

"Wonderful, Lidia! Now turn the paper all around, find some shadow, some area of light or darkness that you want to explore."

"Well, Hyacinthe, I want to draw a toucan. This pointed area right here looks like its beak."

"Fine. Take your fingers and try to emphasize the impression you're getting."

I continued to stroke. My toucan disappeared. In its stead was a robed nun. To the side stood a female torso and in the center leapt a wild horse, rearing up to the heavens.

Suddenly I felt eight years-old. My past had just declared itself. I had stroked out my entire upbringing from a silly cup. My toucan had taken a flight of fantasy and I was suddenly uplifted, introspective and maybe even a potential 'artsy' type.

Hyacinthe: San Diego, California, 1997

I was aboard my boat, working on a project with an acrylic painting, when I heard whining and complaining coming from an attractive woman pulling a dock-cart laden with weekend baggage. I giggled as she tugged and yanked the cart along, dropping things here and there. She must have heard my laughter as she stooped to gather a bag that had fallen near my boat. She looked up and introduced herself as 'Lidia' and asked for permission to come aboard.

I rarely talked to anyone outside the confines of one or another of the galleries I maintained in San Diego. I wished to be unapproachable in my marina milieu, shrouded by plastic from any interference by strangers. I had heard from others at the marina that Lidia was a doctor and I thought she might be someone worth knowing.

I watched as Lidia climbed aboard. She knew the history of my boat, and she proceeded to look around. She quickly opened up to me, sharing experiences, expertise and personal quests. As two professional women discovering a common ground and sharing diverse ideas, we were into every topic conceivable. It surprised me that I could speak so freely to a stranger regarding my concerns about the sad state of so many people who were out of touch with their inner feelings and intuitions.

We discussed our opinions and observations about the deviations in human personality, sociopathic behaviors and negative responses to stress that lead to illness. I had been working on refining a drawing technique to enable and empower adults to access their creativity and Lidia was wondering about illness, regression and repression. Did these two different areas of interest have anything in common?

Eventually, I challenged Lidia to draw: "Then, teach me to draw toucans," she said, displaying a grotesque and garishly colored towel she had purchased during a recent trip to Costa Rica.

"Is she in for a surprise," I chuckled to myself as we established her first drawing session. I guided her through the easy basic exercises. Within twenty minutes, complaining all the while, Lidia had

created a random image of a nun, a female torso and a horse. It was without question, a drawing from childhood memories, images that had been buried in her psyche, suddenly freed.

I believe, at that moment, Lidia realized what she had created was not so much about becoming an artist as it was about something far more profound and mysterious. She was muttering something about my drawing technique facilitating a pathway to creative expression. She questioned me about where it had led some of my students.

And that was how we set out on a quest to formulate a hypothesis for investigating the existence of what was to become the "Silent Stranger."

What Really Happened Here?

During Lidia's first lesson she was able to recognize something essential about the block that occurs in many people during the creative process. During the session she became aware of a judgmental voice telling her how preposterous it was to attempt to create art with charcoal soiled fingers.

Later, Lidia and Hyacinthe elicited an awareness of the same subliminal, judgmental voice in many other subjects. Lidia and Hyacinthe formulated the concept of the "inner-critic" and set out to prove that conscious domination of this controlling voice would be the first key to accessing creativity and meeting one's Silent Stranger: the Adult Creator.

Lidia's drawing (Illustrations 3A and 3B) illustrates the approaches you will learn in order to access your Silent Stranger. The lessons are not mechanical. The success of the technique is based on the capacity to trust the self and act on faith as the inner-critic is confronted and set aside.

To demonstrate Lidia's original idea, we turned her first drawing (Illustration 3A) to its original position and drew a circle

Lidia's First Drawing (right side up)
(Illustration 3A)

Lidia's First Drawing (upside down)
(Illustration 3B)

around the cup. Lidia then turned the cup upside down to find any area that held interest for her and worked on it. You can see an indistinct toucan's beak jutting out to the upper left portion of the drawing (Illustration 3B). The upside-down cup suggested a female torso which immediately attracted Lidia's attention. She ignored the obvious torso and began working on her original intent of drawing a bird. While defining the toucan, she saw something to the far left of her work. She continued to smear and define until a nun materialized. Lidia was subsequently attracted to the upper part of the alleged toucan's beak and smeared charcoal into that area until she thought she saw a horse. She used lines to minimally define her work until she felt confident about expressing the dark area as a horse. Lidia saw beyond the smears and lights and then used lines to provide definition to her rendition. When she realized something creative was happening, she felt comfortable to add flourishes to her rendition. The end result was the expression of an inner vision she didn't fully appreciate until later.

Look at Lidia's drawing. Study the areas of darks and lights, the lines and the smears.

❖   ❖   ❖

The following is a detailed explanation of the process Lidia utilized to access her Silent Stranger. If it is too technical for you at this point, feel free to skim over it. You can return to this explanation later, when a deeper understanding of the theory involved has been achieved. It will serve as theoretical reinforcement for the steps you will encounter as you read and perform the exercises.

Lidia's Steps in Accessing Her Silent Stranger

Action 1: The act of drawing the cup.

Explanation: A simple act, it makes the inner-critic safe to supervise the session. The critic is very vocal at this point.

Action 2: Turning the cup around—turning the paper upside down.

Explanation: This disconcerts the inner-critic as it tries to maintain control.

Action 3: Looking for other points of interest.

Explanation: This momentarily breaks the hold the inner-critic has on the session.

Action 4: Smearing with dirty fingers and accenting the smears with thick and thin lines.

Explanation: This commits the inner-critic to a plan of action. It's very sure it knows what you are going to do.

Action 5: Trying to draw a toucan.

Explanation: The inner-critic attempts to take the easy way out to make you draw something you know.

Action 6: Continuing to move the paper, or point of view, around.

Explanation: This declares a conscious unwillingness to commit to an obvious plan, thereby rebuking the inner-critic.

Action 7: Continuing to stroke and make lines over a now destroyed toucan.

Explanation: Lidia was acting on faith and a commitment to a 'feeling' rather than a commitment to the critic's reality: the toucan.

Action 8: Heavier and more random stroking and blending occurs as confidence builds.

Explanation: As the inner-critic is defied by a sense of creativity, the awareness of being a creator emerges.

Action 9: Continuing to attempt to see by moving beyond the lines, shadows, lights and smears.

Explanation: This instigates the search for a truth, a belief that something is declaring itself, causing the inner-critic to give up its block. The Silent Stranger begins to reveal itself.

Action 10: Defining the drawing.

Explanation: A commitment to a visual statement, the Silent Stranger's method of communication, affirming its accessibility.

Action 11: Studying and analyzing the result, accepting it as one's own by the signing of the work.

Explanation: Finding a rendition from the past, when creativity was initially blocked, provides a sense of empowerment.

CHAPTER TWO

≈

Meet Your Silent Stranger
(The Adult Creator)

The inspiration for the inexplicable drawing is a pristine visitor from the past, the Silent Stranger. Its gifts will be identified as well as the first step in over-coming its enemy, the inner-critic.

The Silent Stranger is emerging from darkness.
It is responding to the distinct prodding signal, a pulling
sensation, as though a hand is stroking it into wakefulness.

As the prodding continues, the Stranger
responds by surveying its expanding domain
and emitting visual concepts to the probing hand that is seeking
     it out.

*". . .What does this have to do with any concept of drawing? . . .
Is this what water feels like? . . ."*

The Silent Stranger responds to the feeling of water.
Another stroke awakens it even farther.
As the moving hand becomes more fluid, the external
input courses inward relentlessly.

The Silent Stranger feels the movement
and settles near the new pathway,
ready to share its life experiences with the path maker.

—LIDIA'S CONCEPT OF THE
AWAKENING STRANGER

The Silent Stranger: Who Is It?

Let's adopt a child's perspective. Here is an actual event, told from a child's point of view. See if you can become engulfed in the child's imagery:

You and I can see it hanging from the rafters at the end of the Yacht Club pier.

Grandfather was very tall, but standing beside the great fish he'd caught, he was nothing... a mere tidbit for a GAPING MAW filled with angry rows of backward angled teeth.

We were both there when they gutted the monster. Grandfather did not shout loud enough or maybe we didn't want to hear.

The wound was bloodless when a too-vigorous helper pierced the entrails and we both saw a tiny, clenched blue hand, followed by an arm, pop out and dangle from the shark's belly.

I knew nothing about birth and it seemed odd that children like you and me were possibly born in the sea. How did we get to land and find a mother and father?

"Some women have babies they don't want." you said.

"But how did the baby get into that fish's belly?" I knew that the truth was imminent.

"It ate the baby whole. Probably for dinner last night." You smiled, but your eyes were riveted on the spectacle and I saw wisdom in your face.

"Oh no! That couldn't possibly be true, because it has huge teeth, and those are meant for chewing. Nothing, nobody swallows their food whole."

I was crying as Grandfather grabbed me by my spindly toothpick arm, and you by your chubby, dimpled elbow and ushered us to the gate.

"Go home this very minute." Grandfather's voice caught somewhere in his throat, and I put my hand out to pat his cheek to make up for the tears I heard in his voice. His eyes were dry and as blue as the sea. A great sorrow was swimming in them, but the meaning of it all was as far removed from my comprehension as the distant horizon which I still imagined could be reached.

There were great mysteries to be discovered at the edge of blue against blue, and I knew when I was bigger than you, like grandmother, I would look to the edge of the earth for wisdom.

Grandmother did just that when she was rocking in her chair on the marbled terrace. I could ask her anything, and she would look off and know the answer.

You continued, lisping through your missing front tooth: "Big fish eat babies that mothers don't want. I told you that already. Grown-ups don't want you to know, but if you're not just perfect and don't keep yourself clean or eat all your food and get good grades... WELL, you might just end up in the same place. AND THEN, when you're in its tummy, it'll be very dark and you'll have to eat what it eats to stay alive."

"How do you get out? Do you tickle the back of its throat so it'll burp?"

"My goodness! You really are dumb! You just walk into its mouth and wait until it opens up. But you better be fast and jump over its teeth. Then you're out and THAT'S THAT!"

Until I went to school and got an encyclopedia, I day-dreamed and dreamt about the maneuvers necessary to exit a shark's belly.

I should have known you couldn't trust a person who lisped.

❀ ❀ ❀

The Silent Stranger is the child's companion. The child's world is a visual world. Fantasy and imagination are primary. Rationalization is secondary.

Creativity, autonomy, self-esteem. We all hunger to possess these qualities. We have forgotten that as children, they were in our possession. We relished each day as we set out to explore our world. Imagination was the only tool we needed to access our creativity, to experience our freedom, to feel worthy of our existence. The process of maturing forced us to abandon this 'unrealistic' spontaneity. As we matured, the demands of adult life became all encompassing and the purpose of one's existence became difficult to appreciate. At times, the purpose could be as simple as getting through the maze of endless daily activities and demands.

Achieving the adult state is a continuous process of socialization. We mature, leaving behind childish behaviors, and learn to function by rules that evolved for the good of the community in which we live. We internalize respected authority figures, as well as the punishing ones. Through these voices of authority, we learned that the simple pleasures and adventures we enjoyed long ago are childish, immature or impulsive: a regression from the process of socialization. If we regress openly, we will be embarrassed. The capacity to be shamed is the point when our innocence is lost.

The internalized authority figure communicates with us through an inner dialogue. This silent voice parrots previous authoritative messages that disciplined our childlike behavior. Its interventions gradually take the form of a subliminal voice, a learned response to outer stimuli that motivates and monitors our daily activities in either a kind or a malicious fashion. The positive aspect of the inner dialogue may be termed the "inner-voice." The negative aspect may be called the "inner-critic."

The inner-critic is protective, as it monitors society's opinion of our conduct. Its concept of shameful comportment incites it to block the open expression of spontaneous behavior. It has no concern with the effect its blocking maneuvers has on our self-expression and creativity, so it can effectively deny the outward expression of our inner imagery.

But... there is a hidden stranger within each of us: an innocent who cannot speak and who communicates through imagery. However, this spontaneous method of expression is blocked by the inner-critic—it is suppressed but waiting to express itself, sheltered in a place where embarrassment remains unknown. The qualities of creativity, autonomy and self-esteem are the Silent Stranger's order of the day. This uninhibited and innocent entity, upon presenting itself to us, is recognized instantly as an old friend, whom we left behind and forgot long ago. Unconditional love and acceptance are the qualities that characterize this friendship, so no expression is too inane or silly to consider. The puzzles that preoccupy a creative mind, in relation to the Silent Stranger become a fascinating, playful mystery of "what-ifs." Complex issues become simple.

We cannot readily become reacquainted with this stranger because our accessibility is blocked by the inner-critic. Very rarely, and with tremendous effort, the stranger escapes from its prison and the spiritual high of self-discovery is experienced.

That escapee is the Silent Stranger.

❖　❖　❖

We were well into our search for the Silent Stranger when Hyacinthe and I were sipping Cuban coffee at one of my favorite haunts. We had just seen an award-winning film, "Bitter Sugar," about Fidel Castro's present day regime. It was written and produced by my friend, Pelayo 'Pete' Garcia. Hyacinthe was eating croquetas for the first time and crying. She was telling me that she was moved by the film even though she couldn't understand a word of it. I thought that her mood was due to the strong coffee and not her temperament since she had informed me incessantly, that she is on the vanguard... a creature well above mundane considerations.

"It was beautiful. I was so touched." Hyacinthe was still reminiscing about the movie. She loudly blew her nose on a napkin, reached into her purse, pulled out a tissue, and daintily dried her tears. "Will he continue to express his marvelous creative spirit, or do you think this was a one shot deal?"

"Pete's an industrial engineer, involved in a black and white sort of career. I used to tease him about being such a conforming yuppie, but look what he's accomplished," I responded between sips of mud-thick Cuban coffee. It was giving me quite a high. When I'm buzzed, it reminds me of the sleepless nights during my residency training, where I had to remain awake for days between catnaps. The great lifesaver was massive cups of prepackaged java. It turned out later to be decafe! Be that as it may, the flavor is Pavlovian: I intellectualize and chatter under its influence.

"He had been looking for deeper meaning in his life," I continued. "While making this film he must have discovered that creative release is like a passion. It's an ecstatic, euphoric, addicting high..." The waiter interrupted my train of thought as he briskly snapped a clean napkin over Hyacinthe's lap. He wandered off to the sitting-room for waiters where he would remain, disdainful and bored, until he sensed some unspoken signal from his hungry wards.

"But to live creatively, you have to release that Silent Stranger which is not always euphoric," Hyacinthe remarked. She had quit crying, and was attempting to look tutorial. She looked like the Cheshire cat from ALICE IN WONDERLAND.

"Yes," she continued. "It's amazing how our search for the

Stranger began with one simple question. I asked you, 'Do you feel there is a part of yourself with which you are no longer in contact?' Remember how all of our art subjects answered that question with a resounding 'yes?' It is exciting to see that people want to find that hidden part! They have a deep yearning to discover what this stranger within them is all about. I love watching them uncover their childhood feelings and innate creativity."

I responded, "And that stranger within seems to have been totally unscathed by the traumas of childhood, relationships, and the sad realities of life. The clue was apparent in the first drawing I did. Remember how I told you that I felt I was on the verge of discovering something really basic? Some mysterious thing seemed to be revealing itself, but then I began to intellectualize to myself about it. Then, just as suddenly, I realized I was drawing things that were important to me when I was about eight-years old."

Hyacinthe said, "You were releasing that part of yourself that was there before you boarded the fast moving train to adulthood. That train, once in motion, couldn't get off the tracks. And once you got aboard, you couldn't get off either. The train was going so fast that, unless you looked straight ahead, everything became a blur. You could become rigid and linear in your thought processes and perceptions. But the capacity to create imagery was intact before you became preoccupied with lines, writing, spelling, and rationalizing. It was your Silent Stranger who expressed itself through imagery. It was fearless, free of guilt, courageously adventurous and joyous. It was neither male, nor female, but had qualities of each. You accessed it through the union between the imaginative innocence from your past and your current adult knowledge. The Silent Stranger then took its place as your adult creator." Hyacinthe's hands were waving through the air in a most emphatic fashion. She was conducting an orchestra only she could hear as she continued with her philosophy.

"This part of ourselves was obviously dismissed as one of the childish things we no longer needed. But, in the mentally healthy adult, it's still intact and whole, merely waiting to be reintroduced to us. As adults, we have to learn to trust its visual imagery."

I naturally rose to the defense of the responsible adult: "I really think that tactile and visual impressions are part of being able to return to this innocence, but it's equally important to remember that it's the present day adult that needs healing."

Hyacinthe's waving overhead has caught the attention of the waiter. He promptly approached and said: "¿Que Señora?" Hyacinthe flatly replied that she didn't want any cake. "¿What you want, Señora?" he said, confused. Hyacinthe folded her hands in her lap and whispered to me, "Tell him to go away until he learns English."

What Significance Does the Silent Stranger Have in Your Life?

We learned to live with a split between faith and knowledge. Experience is a temporary bridge between this chasm. When we act on an unproven belief (faith), the resulting experience permits us to redefine our beliefs as something of which we now have knowledge.

You will begin doing the exercises in Chapter Three as an act of faith. Your experience will help you realize that you have found a tool that bridges the gap between what you know (knowledge) and what you perceive as an unprovable truth (faith). Your Silent Stranger, when released, will emerge with many more choices than when the barriers against its external expressions were incorporated.

Your Silent Stranger will be innocent, but since you are the adult who establishes an accessible pathway for its expression, it will be able to function with your present knowledge and maturity. Old ideas and experiences will be viewed from a new perspective.

Your Silent Stranger will be aware of thoughts, memories, feelings and ambitions that were previously unknown.

You will be able to make creative decisions, create new agendas to meet the demands of daily living, separate real desires from imagined ones and experience a deeper understanding of others. As accessibility to your creative Silent Stranger is enhanced, you will become capable of more complex visions. You will be able to seize power, deal with stress and improve your sense of well being.

The Silent Stranger's only unrelenting enemy is the inner-critic. You will defy the inner-critic with your act of drawing. You will have a tangible record of your growth in your art.

❂   ❂   ❂

My patient was relating the terror he felt about losing control. "Every time I drive along the coastline, I have one of these attacks. The first inkling that I'm in trouble starts with a horrible fluttering in my chest. Then, my hands get clammy, my vision turns into a tunnel and all I can hear is the pounding of my heart in my ears. I feel faint and I have this horrible feeling of impending doom."

"What were you thinking when it first started?"

"I dunno. Maybe I was thinking that the clouds in the horizon were huge tidal waves. I really don't know." There was an introspective, glassy quality to my patient's eyes.

"I want you to put yourself into a situation you know will precipitate your attack. Pay attention to what you are thinking when it starts."

"What are you saying? I'm not doing this to myself. I mean, I'm not stressed," he seemed taken aback, denying that he could be psychologically vulnerable.

"I want you to listen for a little voice commenting in the background. It's there, but you need to have the right mind-set to hear it."

"But I never know when the attack is going to start."

"Pay attention when it does. There is a subliminal commentator, monitoring and perhaps precipitating all of this."

"Are you sure I don't have a heart condition?"

"We've done all the tests: EKG, holter monitor, echocardiogram, and they are all negative."

"All right, I'll try to concentrate, but I can assure you I'm not neurotic or anything like that." He seemed dejected and totally abashed by the idea that his gray matter could be causing an internal warfare against his heart.

Later that day, Hyacinthe and I were sitting on my terrace, watching the sun set into the horizon, an orange fire cutting into the jagged blackness of the hills. As we watched the brilliant streaks extending into the sky I related to her the idea that the inner-critic could be causing panic attacks in one of my most stoic patients. There was something within my patient, some issue, that this inner control freak was trying to buffer.

"Is he in for a surprise! That inner-critic has probably been active for so long, that he doesn't even recognize its existence. Just wait until he faces it!" Hyacinthe rocked deliberately back and forth in the porch swing. Her feet didn't quite reach the ground, so the momentum for swinging had to come from her back and shoulders. Her head bobbed forward first, shoulders and back followed. She was dressed in her traditional black garb, leaving her white framed head glowing and phosphorescent in the descending darkness... the Cheshire know-it-all cat personified.

"Some trauma probably blocked the pathway to his appropriate response to stress. It's amazing that every patient I've had with panic attacks initially refuses to accept the concept of stress as a factor in their heart palpitations. They're always sure they are dealing with life issues appropriately and that their palpitations are caused by some horrible affliction," I pondered out loud.

The sun finally disappeared, and the frogs began croaking frenetically. It became dark and I couldn't see them. There must have been millions of them in the pond universe of my back yard. Their riveting echoes became a part of the night sounds making the darkness seem deeper than it really was.

"The frogs sound like hundreds of metallic rasps, grating and soothing at the same time." Hyacinthe's observations were in tune with my thoughts. "The sun goes down and frogs instinctively know that it's time to gulp air and belch."

At work the next day I received a phone call from my palpitating patient. "You were right. I heard a voice telling me that I was going to drown. It kept repeating, 'You're going to drown!' Then I remembered getting caught in a wave when I was younger. I remembered getting swept across the sandy ocean bottom, and thinking that I would never live through it."

It would have been interesting to involve him in our study in order to make him more aware of his subliminal, vocal companion. Unfortunately, his job took him to another location before we could make firm plans.

A school teacher, who did participate in our study, used the charcoal to stroke out a similar encounter during her first session with us. She was a striking, meticulously composed woman. She looked skeptical as she was told to break a stick of charcoal and smear her manicured hands with the powder. When she was asked to stroke out her feelings about water, there was a visible bracing and tightening of her shoulders and neck. She held the paper rigidly with a her left hand while she stroked the charcoal powder onto the paper in rolling, turbulent waves that enveloped the entire page. As she began to ease into the exercise, her stiff fingers began to relax, her posture changed. A quizzical look, and then a knowing smile replaced it. At that point she was questioned about the significance of her drawing. She related that when she was about eight-years old she had been overtaken by a wave and felt she was going to drown. She could relate the event in elaborate detail, as if it were happening at that very moment. Without fear she related the color of the water as it rolled over her and the sensation of the sand abrading against her as she rolled with the wave. She smiled with this powerful, new knowledge. (Illustration #4)

Your Silent Stranger and Your Inner-Voice

We are not in the habit of listening to our inner-voice. We are often unaware of the origin of our emotional reactions.

Inner dialogue is recognized by the cognitive school of psychotherapy as, "Our inner workings can shut out or twist around the signals from the outside so that we may be completely out of phase with what is going on around us."[1] This school of psychology theorizes that there is a conscious thought between an external event and a given emotional response, but these introspection's (thoughts) are usually not acknowledged on a conscious level.

This concept allows the "therapist to train the subject to focus on their internal dialogue and recognize that a thought links the external stimulus with an emotional response."[2] In other words, an individual has to be trained to listen to themselves.

The inner-voice is a recording of our learned responses to events that occurred and continue to occur as we mature. Since we live with this voice on a daily basis, we don't always hear it. But it's there, and it saves us from having to analyze and process every given situation the moment we experience it. For example, your reaction to a reprimand from your boss is toned down by this voice which allows you to ventilate on a subliminal level by

---

1. Aaron T. Beck, M.D., *Cognitive Therapy and the Emotional Disorders* (New York: New American Library Trade, 1993), 27.

2. Ibid., 27.

Linda's First Mark: Rolling Wave with Eyes
(Illustration #4)

saying something like, *"He doesn't know anything. I've really done a good job. I could just pop him in the nose and walk out of here... but I better not do that. He's the boss, so I'll sit here and take it."* You save the anger for later when you're able to pace, punch a wall and come up with a better plan of action.

This quality of the inner-voice may be described as 'subliminal,' but not 'subconscious.' Its conscious quality is buffered by frequent use, to a level where we don't always hear it.

You can now understand that the inner-voice that modulates your behavior is the pathway of least resistance. It is a learned response that is readily and automatically elicited without your conscious awareness. If you stop and listen, you realize it was there all the time. Its commentary can really be quite amusing during a real down and dirty encounter!

Our contention is that your inner dialogue has both a negative and a positive aspect. The negative aspect is defined as the inner-critic. The inner-critic functions as a block impeding access to your Silent Stranger. If you are a functional adult, removing the block will give you the first step in accessing your Silent Stranger.

You will quickly and easily remove the inhibitions of your inner-critic by permitting yourself to become as a child and dirtying your hands with art material!

❂   ❂   ❂

The marina is an odd conglomeration of people, some who have accomplished all that they want in life, some who are getting there, and some who don't give a damn. The fingers of the five docks extend awkwardly into the water, spiritually elevated on pontoons of alien wood with salt water slapping against them musically, rhythmically. Insults ensue when the slapping between nature and dock gets a bit too aggressive.

Each slip harbors two tenants, usually as alien to each other as

the denizens of the ocean that append themselves to the under surface of the pontoons and pilings holding the dock together. Some
of the boat tenants live on-board, the marina is their home, the
ocean their backyard. A grassy knoll lies above the last finger of the
marina, where the tenants hold grand picnics and parties. Occasionally there is a clash with the homeless of San Diego who consider
the grassy knoll a fair place for a night of rest under the stars.
Guests of the marina hotel walk along the promenade that encircles
the grassy knoll and observe the good life to their left and the bag
ladies to their right.

One day, under a massive tree on the fringe of the grassy knoll,
a homeless young man slept far into the morning. Face to the sky,
arms spread out, legs crossed and sound asleep, he offered reverence
to the heavens. The live-aboard marina tenants walked by, jealous
that his carefree nature permitted him to root himself anywhere
with no preoccupation about work or maintenance of the status-
quo. When the tenants returned from their morning ablutions and
socializing at the marina showers, the young man was still there.
The city of San Diego watered the grassy knoll with powerful
sprinklers sputtering torrents over his rooted form, and still he
slept. Later that day, someone finally decided that the young man
was too quiet, too still and was probably developing bedsores from
not moving. He was quite handsome, but very dirty, so they poked
at him with a stick.

Sirens, policemen, the coroner and an ambulance mourned his
passing. His obituary was muttered by cynical marina tenants for a
few days. The hotel guests went home with a passive tale of having
seen a dead man lying peacefully under a tree in San Diego and nobody noticed for hours on end.

The above tale is true. The point it serves is that we go
through life looking but not really seeing. In later chapters we will
explain how our perception becomes altered and abbreviated. We

usually perceive only a fraction of the whole. This is the well-known principle of being unable to see the forest because of the proverbial preoccupation with the individual tree. By participating in our exercises, you will learn to see. It's important. It could save your life by removing the "b" word (bored) and giving back the joyous wonders of discovery and novelty that make each day an adventure!

Your Silent Stranger: Making Time and Applying Its Lessons to Life's Circumstances

Your Silent Stranger listens to the dialogue between your inner-voice (positive) and your inner-critic (negative). But it cannot help you to act upon the fears or concerns it recognizes in your inner-dialogue unless it has a method of expression. Take time to do the exercises in this book. They will help facilitate a pathway to your Silent Stranger's expression. Learn to discipline that part of your inner dialogue which we've identified as the domineering inner-critic.

Your time is a valuable commodity. These techniques are quick, easy and produce immediate results. We will discuss what is really happening after you have experienced the techniques outlined in Chapter Three. You will want to understand what has happened after you have, in an act of faith, made your mark.

After finishing the first few exercises, subliminal images will suggest themselves. You will probably wonder: *"What is going on? What is happening here?"* Have faith that you will learn to trust and commit to the unseen, not necessarily the obvious.

The important thing to note, at this point, is that the Silent Stranger is readily available and has manifested itself in your first exercise session. The tangible evidence is your drawing. After you complete the exercises you will easily and quickly learn to allow your Stranger to communicate with you.

❀   ❀   ❀

The art of cursing is ancient. Old time magicians invoked curses to cure all that afflicted their minions: lack of love, poverty, impotence, the pox.

Witches used caldrons, magicians used amulets and spells, crusaders used swords, mariners the stars, and modern man. . .

Modern man is afloat, above a sea of mysticism without a curse, a caldron, an amulet, a spell, a star, or a sword... perhaps he dispels his ills with technologic incantations?

A good curse is a cathartic. It dismisses fear, provides strength, embellishes experience with an individual signature, and in general, feels good. It doesn't take any time. It is fast, proficient, powerful, and it sublimates our motivations. The process of sublimation involves transferring one form of energy into another form of action. You take the inner-critic's vociferous energy and override it—silence it—by an invective reply, a strong curse.

Here is a mystical, positive curse: *"I am the creator. No mistake is permanent. I can change anything I don't like."*

We're going to use it... ancient rites, solstice rituals be damned. Modern man cannot spend a lot of time finding lizard tongues, eyes of newt, a good cast iron caldron...

Get ready to have a wonderful experience!

CHAPTER THREE

≈

Drawing Out Your Silent Stranger
The Exercises

You are about to begin a series of easy and fun exercises. These exercises will unlock your natural abilities and help you express yourself with abandon! You will experience a sense of creative freedom and will learn to shut down your inner-critic. The exercises begin with an act of faith, and finish with the development of self-trust. You will take delight in releasing your spontaneous, creative imagination. Then, you will REALLY learn to see.

These are the gifts your Silent Stranger will give to you. So get ready to meet your adult creator!

Getting Ready:
The Tools, Preparation, the Questionnaire, the Blank Page

THE TOOLS:

You may need to buy some items at the art supply or craft store.

1. Paper: white, 8 1/2 x11" typing or drawing

2. Fixative spray: a workable type or hair spray

3. One coffee cup or mug

4. A pencil

5. Charcoal: a dark square stick or soft round compressed stick

6. Eraser: a kneadable rubber

7. Dirty hands

8. Fingertips

9. Imaginary light

10. Imagination

11. Feelings

12. Memories

13. Inner Visions

PREPARATION:

1. Wear dirty clothes or an apron.

2. Set aside sixty undisturbed minutes. If you want to take a break in between, allow yourself at least twenty-minute

periods to do a group of exercises. You can start and stop without interrupting the creative process. You might notice that while engaged in creative activity, where the aesthetic is the guiding principle, time seems to take on a different relevancy.

3. Number your papers, I to 13 on the back in pencil.

4. Find a comfortable place to work, with enough room to spread out the papers.

5. Invite a friend or family member to do the exercises with you.

OBJECTIVES:

1. Give yourself permission to get your hands dirty.

2. Learn to trust yourself.

3. Listen to your inner voice and learn to defy your inner-critic.

4. Use your imagination.

5. Learn to see within.

6. Have fun!

POSSIBLE RESULTS:

1. A desire to throw your drawings away or tear them up—don't do it!

2. Seeing something unexpected in your drawings.

3. Hearing your inner voice acting as a critic.

5. Defying your inner-critic.

6. Getting in touch with your feelings.

7. Drawing out your Silent Stranger.

THE QUESTIONNAIRE

The purpose of this questionnaire is to help you start perceiving as a creator.

1. Can you draw a picture of yourself?

2. Did you draw when you were a child?

3. When did you stop drawing, if you did?

4. Why did you stop, if you did?

5. Do you sometimes feel that you are out of touch with something within you?

6. Do you hear your inner voice as you answer these questions?

7. Is it saying things like: *"This is stupid. I hate tests. What is this all about?"*

8. Would you like to have some fun and learn more about yourself?

9. Would you be willing to remember being a child so you can appreciate being an adult?

10. Do you have an active imagination?

11. Do you consider yourself inhibited?

12. Do you ever see images in clouds?

13. Would you like to meet your Silent Stranger?

THE BLANK PAGE: GETTING IN TOUCH

This blank page is an empty canvas awaiting your creative touch.

1. Rub your clean fingers all over this blank page.

2. Make invisible marks that only you can see.

The marks you make are the beginning of the search. You are getting in touch. You are touching your invisible Silent Stranger. You will now find the courage to make your Silent Stranger visible!

Exercises 1-3

Releasing Your Inhibitions

The following exercises will start you on the path to finding your Adult Creator. You will start by creating expressions of movement with your hands.

Exercise I

Draw the Cup: See How You Draw

PURPOSE: to draw a cup with your current skills.

START:

1. Use paper No. I.

2. Set a coffee cup or mug in front of you.

3. You will draw the cup any way you can, using the charcoal.

   ❧ With the charcoal, draw the cup.

   ❧ Listen as you draw.

   ❧ Do you hear your inner-critic?

   ❧ Is it saying things like: "I don't know how to do this. This is embarrassing. I can't draw."

   ❧ Don't listen to your inner-critic!

FINISH: Laugh at your effort if it amuses you. Later, when you have gained some tools and technique, you will be able to draw a more accurate version of the cup.

SAVE THIS PAPER FOR LATER.

Exercise 2

Fingerprints: Getting Your Hands Dirty

PURPOSE: To ignore your inner-critic and enjoy the freedom of being like a child again.

START: Use paper No. 2.

FINGERTIPS:

1. Break a new stick of charcoal and use small pieces.

2. Rub the charcoal on your fingertips.

3. Make marks: Push down with your fingers and spread the charcoal all over the paper until nothing more comes off.

4. Do it again.

THE CHARCOAL:

5. Put the charcoal on its broad side, press down and make black shapes.

6. Do not make lines: do make shapes.

7. With your dirty fingertips, pull and push through the dark charcoal shapes.

8. Blend the charcoal from the darkest area toward the outside edge of paper.

THE ERASER:

9. Knead the eraser to clean and shape it.

10. Push down and pull eraser through the dark areas in long swipes.

FINISH: Look at your paper. DO YOU SEE ANYTHING?

SAVE THIS PAPER FOR LATER.

Exercise 3

Drawing Water: Going With the Flow

PURPOSE: To create your impression of how water feels. Is it slippery, wet, smooth, cold?

START: Use clean paper No. 3.

DIRTY FINGERS:

1. Smear dirty fingers over paper.

2. Think of how water feels as you smear—slippery, wet, smooth, cold?

CHARCOAL:

3. Use the charcoal to make waves and dark shadows.

4. Blend the charcoal to make a variation of tones.

THE ERASER:

5. Use the eraser to pull light out of the dark tones.

6. Let yourself go with the flow and enjoy.

FINISH: Remember: this is your impression of how water FEELS to you. You do not want to create a picture of an ocean or lake.

SAVE THIS PAPER FOR LATER.

Exercises 4-6

The Basic Technique

You will learn basic techniques which will prepare you to express your inner images on paper.
You will learn to provide depth and definition
to your work by understanding shape, dark and
light, and the line.

Exercise 4

Let There Be Light and Dark: Out of the Shadows

PURPOSE: To use your imagination and light as tools. Enjoy smearing and blending.

START: Use clean paper No. 4. You will not make a picture, just an impression.

AN INNER LIGHT:

1. Imagine a strong light coming from your left, perhaps the sun or a spotlight.

2. Imagine the light is shining on the left side of your paper.

CHARCOAL:

3. With the charcoal, rub heavy dark shadows on the right side of your paper.

DIRTY FINGERS:

4. Blend the charcoal toward the middle and the side with the light.

5. Lightly smear tones toward the left side of your paper.

THE ERASER:

6. Knead and clean and swipe out light from the dark area.

FINISH: You are drawing with an important tool, an inner light projected from your imagination.

SAVE THIS PAPER FOR LATER.

Exercise 5

A Flat Circle, A Round Ball: Light + Dark = Depth

PURPOSE: To take control of light and dark, to create the illusion of depth.

START: Use paper No. 5. You will draw a circle that will appear flat and two dimensional. It may look more like a hole in the paper than a circle.

CHARCOAL:

1. With your charcoal, draw a large circle that fills up the paper.

INNER LIGHT:

2. Imagine a light on your left shining on the left side of the circle.

DIRTY FINGERS:

3. Smear light tones on the left, light side of circle.

CHARCOAL:

4. With charcoal, rub heavy dark shadows and cover the dark, right side of circle.

5. Blend around the circle, dark and heavy on the right, light on the left.

6. Blend the light and dark where they meet in the middle of the circle.

ERASER:

7. Knead eraser to clean it and swipe out one light in the center of the circle.

FINISH: Notice that the flat circle has become a round ball, appearing three dimensional.

SAVE THIS PAPER FOR LATER.

Exercise 6

A Thick and Thin Line: Getting Off the line

PURPOSE: To learn the difference between a line for drawing and a line for writing.

START: Use paper No. 6. You will learn to make a line that is thick and thin using the charcoal stick.

THICK LINES:

1. Hold the charcoal like a pencil at the top of your paper.

2. Press down and drag the charcoal quickly down to bottom of the paper to make a thick line.

3. Repeat, use pressure, and draw a total of four thick lines.

THIN LINES:

4. Hold charcoal like a pencil at the top of your paper.

5. Do not press. Lightly drag to bottom of paper to make a thin line.

6. Repeat, lightly, draw four thin lines.

THICK/THIN LINES:

7. Start with a thick line, release pressure midway, continue on with a thin line.

8. Repeat.

9. Drag the charcoal down slowly and lightly, add pressure midway, continue on with a thick line.

10. Repeat, draw four thick/thin lines.

FINISH: Practice thick/thin lines all over the paper. This is a drawing line that expresses dimension when you are drawing. The thick line shows dark and the thin line shows light. There is a difference between a drawing line and a writing line.

SAVE THIS PAPER FOR LATER.

Exercises 7-8

Expressing the Child

You will learn to express powerful emotions by using the techniques you've acquired. You might find that touch without linear definition is spiritually cleansing.

Exercise 7

The Angry Child: Taking Control of Emotions

PURPOSE: To recall a time when you were growing up and felt anger.

START: Use paper No. 7. Try to remember the feeling of anger as you draw. Be like an angry child. Let go of your restraints, smear impulsively.

DIRTY YOUR FINGERS:

    I. Smear and rub with spontaneous, angry strokes.

CHARCOAL:

    2. Press hard on charcoal with angry feelings and make shapes.

    3. Blend, smear and rub.

THE ERASER:

    4. Use the eraser with abandon.

TAKE CONTROL:

    5. Don't be afraid. Add dark charcoal, smear dirty fingers, blend, erase.

SUBLIMATING INVECTIVE (Remember the curse?):

    6. Say to yourself out loud: *"I cannot make a mistake! I am the creator! I am angry!"*

FINISH: You may be amazed at the sense of relief you feel when you draw out your anger and take control of your emotions.

SAVE THIS PAPER FOR LATER.

Exercise 8

The Fearful Child: Getting Over Fear

PURPOSE: To express memories of fear. Try to remember the feeling of fear as you draw. Let go of restraints, and fall into the fear. Do not try to make a picture.

START: Use paper No. 8.

DIRTY YOUR FINGERS:

1. Smear and rub with fearful, even tentative strokes.

CHARCOAL:

2. Press black charcoal to create shadows around the smears.

3. Blend charcoal with fingertips.

INNER VISION:

4. If an image suddenly appears to you, try to bring it out.

NON-COMMITTAL:

5. You do not have to commit to this image.

6. Continue to add charcoal, smear and blend.

THE ERASER:

7. Use your eraser to create interesting effects.

SEEING IMAGES:

8. To see images in the marks, turn your paper around.

9. Squint, look at light areas, hold the paper away from you.

FINISH: Let your memory of fear guide you. You will know what you fear.

SAVE THIS PAPER FOR LATER.

Exercise 9

Freeing the Adult Creator

You will use the skills you've learned to evaluate your progress by repeating a previous exercise.

Exercise 9

Draw the Cup Again: See How You Draw Now!

PURPOSE: To create another rendering of the cup using the tools and techniques you have gained. When you drew the cup the first time, you might have been prevented from really looking at it because your inner-critic was active.

START: Use paper No. 9. Draw the cup without using lines.

LOOK AT THE CUP:

1. Notice the shape, width, height, any unusual features.

TOUCH THE CUP:

2. Touch the cup with your fingers. Feel the shape, the texture.

DIRTY YOUR FINGERS:

3. Do not use any lines.

4. Smear and blend in the shape of the cup.

INNER LIGHT:

5. Imagine a light shining on the left side of the cup.

CHARCOAL:

6. Press dark charcoal on the right, dark side of the cup.

7. Blend toward the light, left side of the cup.

THICK/THIN LINES:

8. Draw a few thick lines on the dark side of the cup.

9. Draw a few thin lines on the left side of the cup.

FINISH: See the difference: compare your two drawings of the cup.

SAVE THIS PAPER FOR LATER.

Exercises 10-14

Finally, In Touch with the Silent Stranger

You will learn to release the inner-critic by using all your techniques to create a new reality.

Exercise 10
Seeing From Within
EXAMPLE 1: SEE ONE

PURPOSE: To follow Lidia's steps as she does an exercise. Lidia did the exercises long ago. She had become so involved with our research subjects, she hadn't used the techniques after her first few sessions. We put her on the spot by asking her to do the following demonstrations. It only took her minutes to realize the end result. We have delineated the steps and shared her experiences so you may see how the finished impression was created.

Follow Lidia's progress with the accompanying illustrations:

START: Lidia started with an image of a horse in mind. (Illustration #5)

1. Smearing:

    - Lidia dirtied her fingers to smear her first impression.

    - She then captured the attitude of the horse with the tones she had created from the smears.

    - She reminded herself that it didn't have to look like a horse, but it had to feel like one. (Illustration #6)

2. Adding darkness with the charcoal:

    - Lidia then identified where the light was shining on the horse.

    - She put heavier charcoal on the side away from the light.

    - She then began the work of blending and smearing.

3. Adding thick/thin lines:

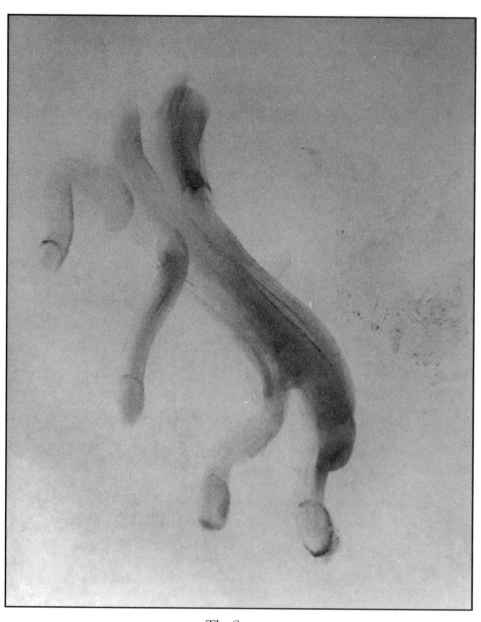

The Smear
(Illustration #5)

More Charcoal
(Illustration #6)

- Lidia added lines to emphasize the form of the horse.

- She then blended and smeared the lines.

4. Using the kneaded eraser:

  - Lidia stroked out light with her clean eraser.

  - She then erased out the form of the horse with the dirt eraser. (Illustration #7)

5. Adding deliberate dark with the charcoal:

  - Lidia then blended the charcoal into the smears.

  - She took away the rigid boundaries created by lines by blending with her fingers.

6. With the side of the charcoal, she created shadows on the horse's form.

7. She blended the charcoal to bring out the form (for instance, the roundness of the horse's rear).

8. Pulling the eraser through, Lidia trusted that a leg would emerge.

9. Not liking the leg, she tried to use the tail to cover it up.

10. Lidia was not happy with the result. What would you do at this point?

11. Finally Lidia did not commit to an image of a horse. She called on her faith to change it. (Illustration #8)

12. The image suddenly looked like a goat, not a horse.

13. Having the trust and confidence to go with another image, Lidia turned the horse into a goat.

14. She then used the eraser to bring out the goat's face and ears. The eraser did all of the work.

15. She added a few thick/thin lines to bring out a few details.

The Dark Horse
(Illustration #7)

Behold A Goat!

(Illustration #8)

17. Lidia smeared and swiped with the eraser to eliminate anything that did not belong with the goat's image.

18. She used the eraser to swipe through and create the illusion of movement.

19. Behold a goat! It could be lying down! It could be jumping!

LIDIA'S COMMENTS: While doing this exercise, I had to remind myself that in my imagining, I am never committed. Initially, it was very difficult to give up the commitment of drawing a horse. But, opening to suggestion, I found infinite possibilities to explore. If I had stuck to the original plan, assuming that the act of having put my hand to the paper was irrevocable, I would have been bound by my own inner-critic and preconceived ideas.

Exercise 10

Seeing From Within:

EXAMPLE 2: SEE ONE AGAIN

PURPOSE: To see the steps Lidia followed to draw a bird from her imagination.

START: Lidia started with the image of a hummingbird in mind.

1. Smearing:

   - Lidia used dirty fingers to smear the impression of the bird.

   - She then imagined that a light was shining on the top of the bird.

   - She added more charcoal to the bottom side of the bird to create shadow. (Illustration #9)

2. Lidia used the clean, kneaded eraser to bring out the form of the bird.

3. She added a few thick/thin lines to define the form of the bird. (Illustration #10)

4. Lidia turned the paper around:

   - She was then able to get a different perspective and more possible images.

   - She saw another bird imposed on the original intended image while looking at the page upside down.

5. She added a few more thick/thin lines to bring out the new image. (Illustration #11)

6. Suddenly, the hummingbird became a bird of prey!

   - Lidia added more charcoal to capture the flowing effect of the wings.

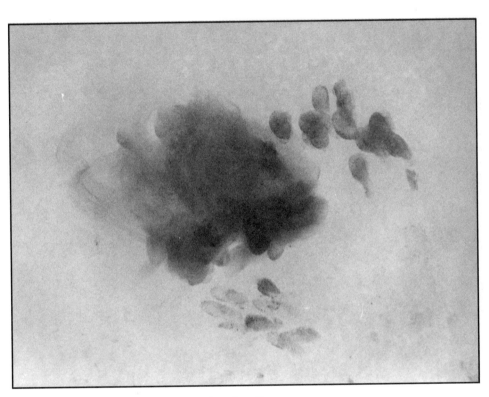

Another Smear
(Illustration #9)

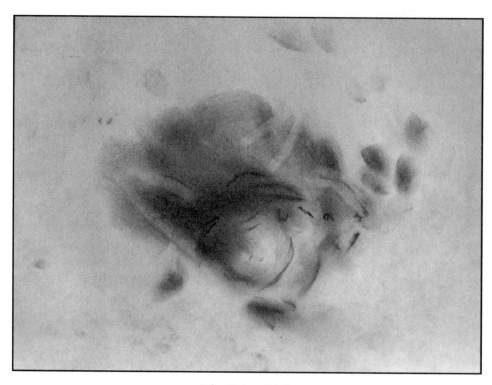

The Other Bird
(Illustration #10)

The Bird of Prey
(Illustration #11)

- She blended the charcoal to eliminate dissonance.

- She then smeared the charcoal to create the effect of feathers.

- She used the kneaded eraser to form the shape of the wings and to indicate that the light came from the front and above.

- She smeared and blended the charcoal.

7. Lidia was unable to complete the bird because she had no idea how a bird's tail goes when it is flying! She made the decision to hide what she didn't know by swiping through it with the eraser to make a blur. She was happy with the result.

8. She then added more thick/thin lines to bring out the wings.

9. Lidia was amazed to discover her hummingbird had become a buzzard!

10. She worked a little further to bring out the skinny, naked neck.

11. She pulled the eraser through to create a sense of movement.

12. She was unsure how to define the buzzard's body so she erased through the wings again.

13. She decided it now looked like a bird of prey swooping down.

14. She used the charcoal to bring out her impression of the buzzard by adding bold strokes to strengthen the impression of wings in flight.

15. She then used the kneaded eraser to create the illusion of

movement while she muttered to herself about the mystery of the position of the tail feathers.

16. While she wondered what happened to the tail, she suddenly saw the claws:

> ❧ She brought out the claws with thick/thin lines. Behold the buzzard! The tail wasn't important after all!

LIDIA'S COMMENTS: I trusted myself enough to realize that what I didn't know about a bird was not the issue. I knew that I could create an impression of a bird. Was I surprised when it became a buzzard—but I felt comfortable and open about going with my instinct.

Exercise 10
Seeing From Within
EXAMPLE 3: SEE ONE, DO ONE

PURPOSE: To find an unexpected image in your work. You will use the drawing tools you have acquired, and you may refuse to commit if you don't like it!

START: Begin with an image of a lion in mind. Use paper No. 10. Since you are not looking at anything, you cannot get the information that you need. You can smear, add charcoal, blend and use the eraser to disguise what you don't know.

1. Dirty your fingers with charcoal.

2. Think of the shape of the lion as you smear your first impression.

3. It doesn't have to look like a lion, it has to feel like one.

4. Add darks with the charcoal:

   ❧ Think of where the light is shining on the lion.

   ❧ Smear with more pressure on the dark side.

   ❧ Put heavier charcoal on the side away from the light.

   ❧ Blend and smear.

5. Add thick/thin lines:

   ❧ Emphasize the form of the lion.

   ❧ Blend and smear the lines.

6. Use the kneaded eraser:

   ❧ Stroke out light with the clean eraser.

   ❧ Erase out the form of the lion with the dirty eraser.

7. Add deliberate darks with the charcoal:

> ❧ Blend the charcoal into the smears.

> ❧ Take away the rigid boundaries created by the lines.

8. With the side of the charcoal, create shadows on the form of the lion.

9. Pull the eraser through the shadows and trust that a leg will emerge.

10. If you don't like the leg, try covering it with the tail or stroke through it with the eraser.

11. If you are not happy with the result do something at this point:

> ❧ Do not commit to the image of a lion if you don't want to.

> ❧ Go ahead and change it to something else. Trust yourself. Go with your instincts.

12. Continue smearing, adding charcoal, blending, erasing.

13. Use the eraser to bring out details and to imply any detail you're not clear about.

14. Add thick/thin lines subtly to continue to bring out detail. Try not to go back on the line.

15. Now use the eraser to eliminate anything that doesn't belong to your image or that you feel uncomfortable with:

> ❧ The eraser is a very special tool. Don't define your final image with it. Use it to subvert the viewer into adding their own detail.

SAVE THIS PAPER FOR LATER.

LIDIA'S COMMENTS: As I did the exercises from my memory of a horse or a bird, I had to keep reminding myself that most people don't see, and therefore don't remember, the whole image of anything. My inadequacies made me happy because they permitted me to explore and suggest rather than define. To be able to define something in detail, I would have to know everything there is about it. To suggest, makes us all learn by having to finish the statement with our imagination.

Exercise 10

Seeing From Within

EXAMPLE 4: SEE ONE, DO ONE, TEACH ONE

PURPOSE: You will overcome your inner-critic by becoming the teacher, the authority figure.

START: Use Paper No. 11

Lets pretend you are a teacher and you have a willing art student. You will play both the teacher and the student.

You will talk to yourself, pretending that you are having a dialogue with your imaginary student to whom you are teaching your new technique. You will have your student do a drawing of a bird from memory. As the teacher, you will impart the same procedures that you experienced learning the techniques, obtaining the tools and doing the exercises. Pretend that your student has completed the exercises in this chapter and knows how to smear and blend with dirty fingers, control light, use charcoal to make dark shadows, use the clean, kneaded eraser to swipe out light and the dirty eraser to pull out form and to create movement and the difference between a thick/thin line used for drawing.

Tell your student to begin with the image of a bird in mind. Remind your student to go with their intuition, begin with faith, and emphasize that they should trust in their spontaneous feelings. Encourage your student to defy the inner-critic and to repeat: *"I can erase anything I don't like. I cannot make a mistake. I am the creator."*

Now become the student. Follow the directions and do this exercise.

1. Smear with your fingers:

   ❧ Dirty the fingers of both hands with charcoal.

- Smear the impression of a bird.

- Imagine a light shining on the top of the bird.

- Smear with more pressure on the dark, bottom side.

2. Use the clean kneaded eraser to bring out the form of the bird.

3. Add a few thick/thin lines to define the form of the bird.

4. Turn the paper around:

  - Get a different perspective and look for other possible images of the bird.

  - Look into the subtle tones you smeared with your dirty fingers.

  - Go with the image of the bird that first appeared to you, although you do not have to commit to this image.

  - If you see another image, another bird or something else, go with those feelings to bring out whatever is imposing itself as you look at the marks. Allow your imagination to create an image.

  - If you still see your original bird, then follow the directions under column A (pages 72-73) for bringing out your original image. If are drawn to another image, or have a feeling that you should smear and blend in another area follow the directions under column B to bring out an idea.

FINISH: Pretend you are the teacher again. Reassure your student of the important things that will be recognized as a result of doing this exercise:

1. Start with faith. You will learn to trust that you are far more capable than you ever believed possible.

2. Spontaneity is necessary in order to be able to commit to a fresh impression of a gesture, form, shape or shadow to create an image.

3. Drawing from the imagination involves memory. If you have never looked intensely at the particular subject that is emerging, there will be very little information to work with.

4. Since there is no specific information available and no point of reference other than reliance on gestures achieved through impulsive smears by erasing and blending, you must rely on creating an impression of the image.

5. Make sure your student repeats the statements: *"I can erase anything I don't like. I cannot make a mistake. I am the creator."*

6. Explain to your student that the Silent Stranger feels the shape and form of the subject.

7. The unexpected images are the Silent Stranger's expressions.

8. If you want to make a copy, take a picture.

SAVE THIS PAPER FOR LATER.

A. The Original Image

1. Add a few more thick/thin lines to define the original image of the bird.

2. Add more charcoal with abandon to capture the flowing effect of wings.

3. Blend the charcoal to eliminate dissonance.

4. Smear the charcoal to create the effect of feathers.

B. The New Image

1. Erase out anything you can't use in your new image.

2. Add more charcoal with abandon and feeling to capture the new image you are seeing.

3. Blend the charcoal to create the form of the new image.

4. Use the eraser to:

- bring out the shape of the new image.

- smear and suggest details that you can't be certain are accurate. In other words, camouflage the unknowns that you can't describe.

- if the unknown is round, e.g., a nose or muzzle, swipe through it with a circular movement; if it's linear, e.g., a tail or a leg, swipe through it by pulling.

- create a sense of movement, pull in a soft, smearing fashion.

A. The Original Image

5. Use the kneaded eraser to:

   - form the shape of wings.
   - indicate where the light is coming from.
   - bring out details.
   - hide anything you don't know by swiping through it.
   - pull through to create a sense of movement.

6. Use more charcoal to bring out the impression of the bird.

7. Finish with a flourish, with the eraser or the charcoal, accent a wing or whatever pleases you.

B. The New Image

5. Use more charcoal to emphasize the image.

6. Complete the new image with a flourish, to add your own original touch.

Exercise 11

Final Marks: Are You Going to Meet A Stranger?

PURPOSE: To clean your dirty fingers and continue your exploring, going with the flow and leaving yourself open to the possibilities of new images that may appear. Remember, when you least expect it, you will get in touch with your Silent Stranger.

START: Use paper No. 12.

1. Wipe, smear and rub your dirty fingers on your paper until no more charcoal comes off.

    Take a final look at the marks you made while you were wiping your dirty fingers on your paper. Intent on cleaning your hands, you were not trying to draw anything. Look at your marks for a moment. There was no image in mind, yet you might see something. It may pop out at you, insisting that you declare it. If some thing appears, go ahead and try to bring it out.

    Now you are creating images that are free expressions. You are impulsive and having fun as you are adding flourishes, seeing images, smearing, blending and erasing. If you continue to access the pathway the exercises have facilitated, you will do better and better. Who knows, when you least expect it...!

2. What is left on your fingers is a residue that wipes off. When done, clean your dirty hands with a moist towelette or soap and water.

3. Charcoal is harmless and can even be eaten to eliminate flatulence.

4. Charcoal is not a permanent medium and will not stain anything.

5. When using charcoal you cannot make a mistake, because it will erase easily.

6. You must fix your drawing with workable fixative or hair spray to make it permanent.

Exercise 12

Destroy the Cup, Not Your Ego

PURPOSE: To allow the ego to enjoy the satisfaction of what you have made and then EXPAND your ability to perceive things in greater detail.

START: Use paper No. 9.

THIS IS A SYMBOLIC ACT:

1. Turn the paper around so the drawing of the cup is upside down.

NOW, TAKE AN OPPORTUNITY TO SEE SOMETHING ELSE:

2. Squint.

3. Look within the subtle tones for images to suggest themselves to you.

4. Hold the paper and drawing away from you.

5. When something suggests itself, add darks with charcoal.

6. If nothing presents itself, add dark at random.

7. Blend.

8. Pull the eraser through the darks and marks.

TO BE FREE TO REALLY SEE:

9. When you see something, add thick/thin lines in a few places, so others can see what you see.

10. You don't have to describe everything with line. Give others a chance to be free to see what you see. You need only barely indicate what appears to you.

11. Show, but don't tell. Let the viewer feel and see according to their interpretation.

Exercise No. 13
The Papers You Saved

PURPOSE: To bring forth new images from the random marks you made on the papers you saved. You are about to discover hidden images, as you continue to work on the drawings! You will take your cue from the examples set forth in the exercises. You will use the tools you have gained.

START: Go back to the papers you saved:

1. Spread them out and pick one to work on.

2. Set the other papers aside.

3. Look at the marks you've made on the paper.

If you see an image:

> ❧ Use the tools you've learned to define it.

> ❧ As you work, if you find you are not happy with the emerging image, change your perspective by moving the paper around or upside down.

> ❧ Continue to define any area that attracts your attention by adding charcoal. Pull the eraser through the marks and shapes to bring out light, to define, or to camouflage unknowns. Add lines for embellishment or definition.

If you don't see an image:

> ❧ Squint, turn the paper around and even upside down. Do not try to assemble all the smears into an image. Look for shapes within the light, medium and dark toned areas. DO NOT try to assemble the entire paper into one image unless one is obvious.

> ❧ When you have identified an area of interest, proceed as above in "If you see an image."

USE ALL YOUR TOOLS:

1. Add motivation and inspiration.

2. Add a new sublimating invective: *"I only want to please myself. I don't care. Other's opinions don't matter when it comes to my own personal creative expression."*

3. Now that you understand the techniques, you might want to go back to, "Lidia's Steps in Accessing her Silent Stranger" in Chapter One, and compare your steps to hers.

4. Do not be afraid to declare it, and share it!

5. Repeat the above exercise at your leisure with the other papers you saved.

Exercise 14
I Did This Drawing!

PURPOSE: To find your Adult Creator's signature.

Until this moment, you have been anonymous. You were merely doing childish things with dirty hands. You heard your inner-critic loud and clear, as it repeated all the restraining messages from long ago. You acted on faith and ignored your inner-critic by stating that you could erase anything you didn't like, that you could not make a mistake, that you were the creator! You obtained the tools, techniques and confidence to express yourself. Images appeared that you did not deliberately intend to make, and you were able to elaborate on those images to express what you were seeing. Through the essence of acting on faith, refusing to commit, and developing self confidence, you got in touch with your Silent Stranger!

This was enabled by the fact that, until this moment, nobody took responsibility for these drawings, because—nobody had signed them.

START: Prepare to claim the drawings as your own. Your inner-critic is probably having a field day with this! It may be screaming: *"Don't you dare! You don't want anybody to know who did these. What will people think if they see the mess you made? You couldn't draw before and you can't draw now!"*

In spite of what you may be hearing, isn't there a little feeling of satisfaction? Maybe a small inner-voice is suggesting, *"Some of the drawings aren't that awful. I may not have intended to draw the images that turned up, but I kind of like them."*

Go ahead. Sign the drawings. But first, you need to find a more artistic signature, don't you think? You may not want to sign your art with the perfect penmanship you use to sign your checks.

START ON ANY PAPER:

1. See how you sign your name. Write your usual signature on the line below.

   _____

2. Now try signing your name in a different direction on the line below.

   _____

3. Now try stretching your signature up and down with flourish, on the lines below.

   _____

   _____

   _____

   _____

   _____

   _____

   Practice your new signature! When you feel comfortable with it, use it to sign your drawings. When you sign each drawing, claim it, name it, even frame it!

CHAPTER FOUR

≈

Facilitating A Pathway

The inner-critic is the block to accessing your Silent Stranger. Establishing a well-traveled pathway to your Stranger allows you to expand on its powerful gifts.

You are led

Through your lifetime

by the inner learning creature,

the playful spiritual being

that is your real self.

Don't turn away

from possible futures

before you're certain you don't have

anything to learn from them.

You're always free

to change your mind and

choose a different future, or

a different

past.

—RICHARD BACH

How You Created a Pathway

Repetition is the key concept in creating a mental pathway to your Silent Stranger. The more times you perform a skill, the easier it becomes. In the process of performing the previous repetitive exercises you have opened the door to an expressive passageway that is not based on a verbal skill, but on a deeper and more creative, communication skill.

The process of dirtying your hands, acting on faith, focusing on a finite space, and flowing with the essence of the exercises utilized your inherent motor skills and emotional makeup in a novel fashion which disconcerted your inner-critic. You may have been thrown off guard initially because you were not given a visual image to copy. This was intentional. It was meant as a break from a pattern of using external stimuli as a source to draw from.

The suggestions in the exercises were repeated while advancing the demands on basic motor and visual skills. You repeated the reminders—the sublimating invectives—of your infallibility, *"I can erase anything I don't like. I cannot make a mistake. I am the creator."*

The path to the Silent Stranger depends upon your capacity to set aside the preconceived ideas that your inner-critic tries to impose on you. The inner-critic tries to block you from accessing the imaginative, adventurous part of your nature. The more pressure the inner-critic puts forth, the more adamant should be your words—your sublimating invective: *"I can erase anything I don't like. I cannot make a mistake. I am the creator."*

This is your pathway to the Silent Stranger. Make sure you travel upon it frequently. You do not have to become an artist to employ the techniques. If you don't have time for the charcoal exercises, you can imagine your fingers stroking the paper. Silently repeat the mantra to access your creativity and experience the dynamic power of your friend, the Silent Stranger. (Illustration #12)

If you feel compelled to change the invective to better suit your needs, use your imagination to find your own verbal key to the Silent Stranger.

It's almost too easy—but you must have found out by now, that the most rewarding realizations are simple!

What Does It Mean?

If a concert pianist has learned his music well, it flows to the eaves with flawless splendor. All desire and expectation is mute as the hands take over for the mind. All study that elicited technique and theory is banished as the learned pathway delivers the performance. On occasion, interrupting the delivery might break the spell. The mind may take over again and the beautiful music is lost.

A young child has a stomach ache. Her mother tends her with fresh sheets, chicken soup and fairy tales. This nurturing leaves a warm, dependent feeling that overpowers the misery of illness. Subsequently, during times of stress, the need for this attention and affection may become so great the stomach ache may become automatic. The child, now grown, might translate psychological mayhem into a physical complaint. The stomach groans and the adult takes ill. What pleasure to return to the lilac world of fresh sheets and chicken soup, absolved of all responsibility! The nurtured child had facilitated a pathway to obtain relief from life's demands: a learned pattern of behavior with positive reinforcement to a negative inciting stimulus.

Establishing Access by Repetition: A Facilitated Pathway

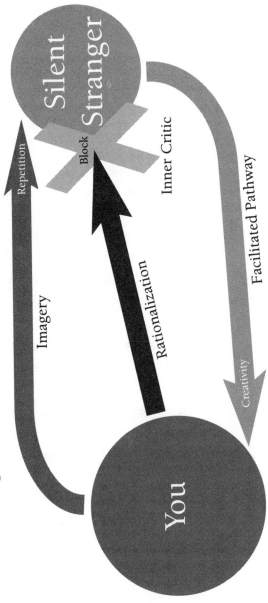

Facilitated Pathway: the interaction of the inner critic and the Silent Stranger:

- Utilizing imagery in a repetitive manner permits access to the Silent Stranger
- Rationalization stimulates the inner critic causing a block to accessing the Stranger
- Accessing the Silent Stranger permits overt manifestation of creativity

(Illustration #12)

These examples are methods of facilitating a pathway. The effort was conscious in the pianist, unconscious in the young child. The end result, outward expression of a learned behavior, was the same. The essential tool in both pathways was the same: repetition and reinforcement. The outward expression of the learned behavior became automatic. The common thread was the absence of intellectualizing or rationalizing while expressing the behavior.

From infancy, the process of maturing involves learning tasks that will eventually become automatic. It would be difficult to recall the intellectual effort involved in initially learning to ride a bicycle, button a shirt, or tying one's shoes. As a task is repeated, the performance of that task requires less and less intellectual input as a pathway has been facilitated to demonstrate the skill.

If a learned skill is not utilized, it risks becoming lost. You may need to think about individual parts of the skill in order to demonstrate it. Performance is affected until an automatic pathway is again established.

The childhood acceptance of a statement on blind faith is cemented with visual imagery, not by the reasoning quality of a mature adult. As a child becomes older, visual imagery becomes secondary and rationalization primary, in reinforcing life's lessons: The Silent Stranger gradually withdraws. As an adult, the reasoning process replaces the child-like blind faith. Intellectualizing develops and eventually provides the whys and wherefores of the "don'ts."

Hyacinthe's tale of panty burning emphasizes this point. She confided one day that she always has an image of a house afire when she purchases new lingerie. An absurd thought? Not really. Hyacinthe remembers as a small child, being interrupted during play by her mother's command, "Put your clean panties in the..." Little Hyacinthe was distracted with play and was not paying attention. She was close to the oven, so she put her nicely folded panties in there. In her mind, she had done as she was told and put the panties into something. Moments later, her frantic mother screamed, "You put your panties in the oven? The whole house could have caught on fire!"

Lidia, on the other hand, recalls an incident when she threw a paper from a moving car and was scolded by her mother, "Don't throw things out of the window. You will blind someone!" What ensued was the image of a person being blinded by the act of throwing a piece of paper out of the car.

By the time that Hyacinthe understood the mechanisms of the oven—you turn it on, it gets hot, something can burn, and Lidia understood that paper can land on a car windshield, obstructing the driver's view, the Silent Stranger had been relegated to its role as a jailed convict in the recesses of the subconscious

Is this Silent Stranger a part of yourself... lost long ago? The answer is yes! It has been alluded to by many psychotherapists. As our social order expands from family, to peers, to authority figures, the critic becomes more predominate. The individual encounters conflict by denying (repressing) the subliminal parts of his nature, essentially blocking the Silent Stranger. C. G. Jung in THE UN-DISCOVERED SELF, speaks of the individual and society "...his instincts not only attach him to the macrocosm; they also, in a sense, tear him apart, because his desires pull him in different directions. In this way he falls into continual conflict with himself and only very rarely succeeds in giving his life an undivided goal—for which, as a rule, he must pay very dearly by repressing other sides of his nature."[1]

The inner-voice is relevant to the individual and his or her place in the social structure. It is not to be totally discarded nor

---

1. C. G. Jung, *The Undiscovered Self* (New York: Little Brown, 1957).

overruled, only the part that is the inner-critic. The inner-critic, the block, must be defied in order to access the adult creator, your Silent Stranger.

To facilitate a pathway to creativity, this critic must be acknowledged and confronted. Acknowledging, in an affirmative voice, that there can be no mistakes, only a process of creation and correction, silences the critic.

Your Inner-Critic: The Ploy of Commitment

Lidia was playing Malagueña on the piano. She was cursing every few seconds. This was a piece she had learned to play at her grandmother's ninetieth birthday.

"Did you know that the composer, Lecuona, was Cuban?.. A Cuban with a pituitary disorder," Lidia ranted. "Nobody has such a large finger span. There is simply no way to reach all of these stupid chords."

"Tell your inner-critic to shut up," Hyacinthe yawned. "You play beautifully."

"Not true! I played this piece better when I was twelve years old. The more I dissect it, the worse it gets. If I don't think about it I can play it fine, but then I imagine all the mistakes I'm going to make. So I'm tearing it apart note by note, chord by chord." Lidia complained.

"It sounds great to me. Did you know that I taught myself to play? I've been told by a piano teacher that the composers must be turning over in their graves, because there is no resemblance to what I play and what they wrote. I don't care! I love to play!"

"So do I, but I don't play by ear. I have to study, and study. If I can't play it right, I won't play it at all," Lidia replied.

"Well then, your inner-critic certainly despises piano playing," Hyacinthe replied.

❀   ❀   ❀

Commitment to rules is a ploy the inner-critic utilizes to block access to the uninhibited self. That is its attempt to keep things safe and under control.

The critic is that part of the inner-voice which internalizes negative connotations to certain acts. This implies that an individual's performance was formerly met with negative feedback. The inner-critic, in an attempt to protect the individual concept of self, developed dialogue to prevent the damaging behavior from repeating itself.

The inner-critic monitors for control so that ego-damaging behavior does not become overt or readily obvious to the conscious self or to others. It is apparent just below a conscious level of dialogue and can be heard to criticize when an individual is presented with a potentially ego-damaging situation. The individual feels relief at being spared an embarrassment and relies on the inner-critic in situations where the performance of an overt act might bring ridicule or censure.

Setting Your Inner-Critic Aside

John Steinbeck, a Nobel prize-winning author, made allusions to an inner-voice. He used the existence of an inner dialogue in Sweet Thursday to dramatize one of his character's alienation from his surroundings. The tone of this book is whimsical and humorous. The character, a marine biologist named Doc, spoke to himself through a conscious voice, a lower voice, and an emotional voice. The lower voice was a chastising voice that belittled Doc's discontent with his current status in life and his inability to write a scientific paper about "apoplexy in octopuses." When Doc overcame his lower voice, he broke from his set pattern of compulsive behavior and found happiness and worthy qualities in a hooker who loved him. Steinbeck wrote a whole novel on Doc's ability to confront and defy his mean spirited inner-critic!

Initially Doc's critic subverted him by breaking into his conscious thoughts while he was studying sea plankton under the microscope. "What lovely little particles, neither plant nor animal, but somehow both," said Doc's conscious voice. The inner-critic responded with, *"What are you looking for little man? Is it yourself you're trying to identify? Are you looking at little things to avoid big things?"* Doc did not deny hearing this demeaning inner-voice. He took the first step in setting aside the inner-critic by acknowledging the critic's existence.

Later in Steinbeck's story, Doc undertook the second step in understanding how to deal with the inner-critic when he heard a voice coming from behind him. He had quit searching for marine specimens and was involved in little-boy reverie by digging a hole on the sandy beach. A voice stated, "There are no clams here." Doc's response was, "I know it," as his intellectual voice screamed he just wanted to be left alone. He had identified the critic. He deemed the personless voice to be a crazy annoyance, a "bughouser."

Doc's third step was to actually set the inner-critic aside. He rolled back on his heels and arrogantly challenged the voice. When he turned around, the voice who had proclaimed itself as a 'seer' now belonged to a bearded stranger with 'the lively, innocent eyes of a healthy baby.' The stranger invited him to dinner and proceeded to relate, "I live alone... I hear the waves at night and see the black patterns of the pine boughs against the sky. With sound and silence and color and solitude, of course I see visions. Anyone would." Doc's Silent Stranger, previously blocked by the inner-critic, had revealed itself!

When doing the exercises, you are following the same steps as Doc:

STEP ONE: **Accept the inner-critic's existence.** The exercises insult the inner-critic's need for an orderly environment with charcoal powder and grit. The negative banterings reveal the critic's existence.

STEP TWO: **Identify the inner-critic.** Making a mess of tones and shades by smearing is a childlike act. The inner-critic will protest loudly in an attempt to have the orderly adult resume control. Identifying the blocking quality of the critic's voice is essential.

STEP THREE: **Set the inner-critic aside.** The act of stroking out anger and fear is an initial inciting agent for the inner-critic's ploys. Once the inner-critic is acknowledged and identified, it must be sublimated. The process of sublimation involves transferring one form of energy into another form of action. You must take the inner-critic's vociferous energy and override it—silence it—by an **invective** reply, which implies a strong denunciation. The phrases, *"I can erase anything I don't like; I cannot make a mistake; I am the creator,"* are our suggested sublimating invectives, because they are both forgiving and empowering at the same time.

Exercises for Listening to Your Inner-Critic

If you have difficulty listening to, or even hearing your inner-critic, we have included some exercises which will make its presence apparent, or at least make the volume of its protest louder!

Through the Looking Glass: Bringing Out the Inner-Critic

PURPOSE: You will expose your inner-critic and set the critic's ego defense mechanisms aside.

START:

1. Fetch a mirror.

2. Look at yourself.

3. Study your features and your expression as you are looking at yourself.

4. Go ahead, lie to yourself if you must. Tell the mirror how beautiful or handsome you are.

5. What are you are doing?

   - Are you repeatedly drawn to what you consider are your negative attributes?

   - Are you making a face?

6. Listen closely, there is a subliminal voice dominating your observations. Defy it! Whatever you feel like doing, do something else:

   - If you're drawn to stare at your mouth, stare at your eyes or your nose.

   - If you feel compelled to make a funny face, mimic how you look when you're angry, or vice versa.

7. Do you recognize your whole face, or just the (perceived) pleasant or unpleasant parts?

8. Stare at your nose, and then your teeth.

   - Is the voice getting louder, telling you that you need a nose job, or extensive dental work? You are now approaching the area where the ideal-self and the real-self are in conflict.

9. Confront the inner-critic and accept the perceived defect noting that you can change anything if you're so inclined. It's your decision—you could have a nose job, or extensive dental work if you really chose to do so.

10. When you have accepted the negative, the inner-critic will quiet down.

Through the Rabbit Hole: Setting Up a Dialogue With Your Inner-Critic

PURPOSE: You will imagine a hole in the ground. Your task is to go through the hole. Your inner-critic will want you to take the easy way out. It will monitor the safety of each step you choose. Be reckless, or logical. It's your choice!

START:

1. There is a hole in the ground.

   Choices: The inner-critic, the protective authority figure, might be saying, "why should I crawl into a hole in the ground?" The imaginative self, the explorer and fearless conqueror, wants to explore the hole.

2. How deep and how wide is it?

   Choices: The inner-critic will make it shallow and safe. The imaginative self will make it come out on the other side of the world, perhaps in China.

3. Is it light or dark?

   Choices: The inner-critic will want there to be light. The imaginative self may want to get sucked through a vortex of darkness.

4. How will you get through it?

   Choices: It's your turn to figure out which choice the inner-critic and the imaginative self will make by listening to your own inner dialogue:

   ☙ Will you go in voluntarily, or will you fall in?

   ☙ Will you squeeze through it or will you get stuck?

5. What will you find at the bottom?

6. How will you get out?

   Choices: You can stay there forever, if you choose... or maybe you took a ladder with you.

Why Can't I? It's Mine! The Childhood Room

PURPOSE: To give an example of the internalization of authoritative do's and don'ts that matured into a dominating inner-dialogue (inner-voice/critic). You will imagine your childhood bedroom. You are going to make it your personal domain with no authority figure in command.

START:

1. What's in your room?

   Choices: The inner-voice/critic will want an orderly room with everything dusted and in its place. The imaginative self will want rocks, experiments, bugs, etc., readily accessible and strewn about.

2. What time is bedtime?

   Choices: The inner-voice/critic will want an early bedtime so that you can grow big and tall. The imaginative self will make bedtime when there is nothing else to do.

3. What do you do in the dark after the lights are out?

   Choices: The inner-voice/critic will want you to go right to sleep. The imaginative self will look under the bed for monsters, make a sheet tent and continue the day's activities unabated.

4. Are you afraid of the dark?

   Choices: The inner-voice/critic will soothe away fears by becoming the protective adult. The imaginative self will use a flashlight to laser the bug-a-boo to death, thereby conquering all fear.

   Note: This is a very important consideration. In childhood, the authority figure is protective as well as the boundary-setter. When the adult authority figure steps in and helps conquer nighttime monsters they are protecting the fearful child. This reinforces the internalization of the inner-voice, the protective crusader for the adult/child.

5. The room is yours! There is no authority figure telling you what to do.

   Choices: You can have mortal combat with monsters, draw on your walls, or tap dance on the dresser. Feels good, doesn't it? The protective inner-voice will pick conservative alternatives. Debate with it while it tries to make you keep your room neat and tidy.

Further Inner-Critic Exercises, If You Need Them

If you have a clear concept of your inner-critic and have heard it relentlessly harping at you, you might not need to pursue these other exercises. If you still find it is somewhat elusive, you can create further exercises on your own.

You might try picking a topic that motivates you in a 'what if' category. For example, When you were a child did you pretend to be a superhero, movie star or great dancer? What would your inner-critic say if you pretended to be any of those things now? Take notes of the inner-dialogue that rejects your fantasy choices: *"You can't be a... (superhero, movie star, great dancer) because you're too... (fat, ordinary, awkward)... and, people will laugh at you."*

Another good topic to conceptualize the inner-critic would be to rewrite your life story and elaborate upon any 'what ifs' that come to mind. You are guaranteed there will be an internal debate and the chairperson will be the nosy, self-appointed inner-critic!

After practicing the inner-critic exercises you will recognize the blocks that the inner-critic has developed against your adventuresome, creative Stranger. By ignoring the inner-critic's banter, you will learn to appreciate details and innuendo that previously eluded you—you must now learn to really see.

CHAPTER FIVE

≈

Accessing the Silent Stranger in Your Daily Life

Life's challenges acquire a new perspective when you share your experiences with your Silent Stranger.

Although he has no form
my eyes saw him
and his glory shines in my mind,
which knows his secret
inner form
invented by the soul.
What is beyond the mind,
has no boundary.
In it our senses end.
Mukta says: words cannot contain him,
yet in him all words are.

—MUKTA BAI

(13th century)

Improving the Quality of Your Life Experiences

*M*any people simply do not really see. When they look, they focus on certain aspects of a visual stimuli and they don't perceive the whole in detail. Reality, if defined by what we see, becomes an individual matter of perception.

Horace Miner, an anthropologist, wrote an article entitled "The Body Rituals of the Nacirema." The Nacirema society was based on a sado-masochistic culture. The natives scoured the inside of their mouths with bore hair bristles, baked their heads inside of ovens once every lunar calendar month, and visited Holy mouth men who used awls to make holes in their teeth. They were also extremely superstitious. Each abode had a holy absolution font where the natives kept potions given to them by the Medicine Man. Even though these potions were often no longer effective, the natives were afraid to throw them away for fear they would need them in the future. They kept these old amulets in a special cabinet.

What a horrible social structure, but... surprise! *Nacirema* is *American* spelled backwards! Dr. Miner took parts of our culture and put them together to make a skewed impression of the whole.

Carlos Castaneda, another anthropologist, studied a Yaqui Indian sorcerer's concept of "really seeing." Unfortunately don Juan, the sorcerer, espoused seeing with the assistance of hallucinogens, in particular mescalito. In A SEPARATE REALITY, Carlos says to don Juan: "But if the same tree changes every time you *see* it, your *seeing* may be a mere illusion."

Don Juan's response: He laughed and did not answer for some time, but seemed to be thinking. Finally he said, "Whenever you look at things you don't *see* them. You just look at them, I suppose, to make sure that something is there. Since you're not concerned with *seeing*, things look very much the same every time you look at them. When you learn to *see*, on the other hand, a thing is never the same every time you *see* it..."

If the act of seeing is focused upon qualities that are of interest, many aspects of the whole may be ignored. Our perception of the whole is superimposed with innuendoes as we evolved from a blank slate to a voluminous tome of experiences.

Learning to perceive with a clean slate will revitalize the quality of our experiences with the intensity we enjoyed before we realized our own fallibility. Seeing beyond the obvious while attempting to interpret with a new outlook, emphasizes individual experiences and accesses our imagination.

With this in mind, the simple activities of daily living become a panorama of possibilities! Removing preconceived and limited details permits a new approach to even the most mundane task. For example:

- Try to imagine the universe of life in the dust ball you uncover as you clean house. See how quickly time goes by when you discard the concept of 'the task' and become enmeshed in 'the adventure.'

- Look at the scenery as you travel to and from work. Imagine what might have been happening around you 100 years ago, 500 years ago.

- As you have breakfast, imagine where the fruit or grain

came from. Think about the process it went through to get to your table.

- As you walk by strangers, smile at them as if they are old friends. Imagine that you have genuinely warm feelings for them as fellow compatriots.

If you practice, the Silent Stranger will deluge your daily life with visual images that give new meaning to your experiences. Your inner-critic will try to dissect this innovative manner of seeing and place it in a learning perspective. Block that moderator by continuing to receive new, enhanced visual images! While you are in this mode, don't permit an internal dialog unless you wish to act upon the visual image to create new goals.

Creativity

In his book, CREATIVITY AND PSYCHOLOGIC HEALTH, Frank Barron states, "The creative genius may be at once naive and knowledgeable, being at home equally to primitive symbolism and to rigorous logic. He is both more primitive and more cultured, more destructive and more constructive, and occasionally crazier and yet adamantly saner, than the average person."[1]

Barron's statement expresses the dualism of the creative person. To be creative, you must be free. Don't give up your hard-earned morals, but accept that you have internalized the authority figures that surrounded you as you matured. You are still shrouded with the 'do's and don'ts' of these figures who now exist in the form of the inner-critic—the past is present in that vocal raconteur. Analyzing whether it is constructive or destructive is irrelevant. So what if an authority figure was harsh or abusive? What relevance does

---

1. Frank Barron, *Creativity and Psychologic Health*, (New York: C.E.F. Press, 1990), 224.

that have now? Doing battle with the past prevents progression in the present! Get rid of the critic! Now you have a tool of power with which to access your inventiveness, originality, creativity. You will see into a new reality with this unique perspective!

Expressing your creativity is not easy. When you did the exercises in Chapter Three, you may have found yourself alone in a room. There was no voice of authority directing your activity. You made an autonomous decision to please only yourself and you became, at that moment, the creator and possibly the defiler. There may have been a nagging inkling that you felt inadequate or unable to manifest what you were wanting to express.

Then, at some point, you may have realized that you were not alone. Your inner-critic was your private companion in the room. It emphatically let you know that your perceptions were one thing—but laying your hands on a primitive smeared picture would defile it. It told you that you were incompetent to create and define an impression of a visual image. It tried to take away your sense of trust in your innate skills and attempted to reinforce the rules. It was undermining your belief in yourself as a creator.

Your former authority figure may have reappeared and berated you, *"what if someone sees what you have created and thinks it is childish or ugly?"* But you persevered, gathered your courage, acted on faith, and strove for a mode of expression that came from within you.

In the act of creating, you may have come to realize that you shouldn't become involved in the concept of beauty just for the sake of beauty. To demonstrate this point, look at the random smears you have made in the exercises. Some of the shadows and lines are beautiful without a preordained thought of creating beauty. Remember, however trite, that 'beauty is in the eye of the beholder.'

As you worked through the exercises your perception was altered. Each experience was embellished as if it was new and had never been experienced before. The magical, wonderful world of 'what ifs' presented itself.

In the process of seeing things from a different perspective, a mundane problem might become a fascinating mystery to solve. Applying the open ended 'what if?' accesses the Silent Stranger's gift of imagination. The solution to a problem will be viewed— seen—rather than verbalized. The inner-critic must learn that your creative act is not ego-threatening even though it might be innovative.

This requires repetition: seeing in a creative way in many different situations. As the inner-critic experiences positive reinforcement, creativity is more readily accessed. The inner-critic's capacity to deviate from the status-quo becomes easier.

Starting with simple 'what ifs' will lead to a greater capacity to be creative with difficult concepts. Be daring and courageous!

Relief From Stress

The act of being creative renders order where there was chaos. Chaos is stressful. But a certain degree of chaos is essential to motivate us into action. If there was no chaos, life would be an endless monotony of sameness.

Stress is part and parcel of our existence. The relevant issue is how we deal with it. If we are out of touch with our motivations, our goals and aspirations, a common affliction ensues: anxiety. Stress that is left unchecked is magnified by irritability, tension and a generalized feeling of uneasiness and anxiety.

Free-floating anxiety is a condition that indicates an individual is no longer aware of the causes of his or her discomfort. Internally, chaos, runs rampant. Thoughts and motivations are no longer clear, or are ridiculed by the inner-critic as it tries to find a logical, previously successful method of controlling the discord.

Drawing on the Silent Stranger, and using its visual imagery method of communication, removes the need to inspect and analyze. A perfect example of this relates to one of our subjects smearing out a very reasonable rendition of an owl without recognizing what he had done until he stood back from his drawing. The degree of anxiety and stress might require time out, dirtying one's hands with charcoal and stroking out feelings of passion, anger, fear or doubt. A functional adult will use this technique to draw comfort from their own uniqueness. No problem is beyond their control. They are capable of restoring order from chaos.

An adult, advanced in the technique of accessing their Silent Stranger, might find the answer to their stress within their drawings. They could formulate a plan of action to correct the stress/anxiety inducing factor.

Mind-Body Harmony

Unrelenting stress, coupled with a perceived inability to change undesirable circumstances, causes a physiologic response to the stress. The autonomic nervous system, the fight or flight master of our physical being, is stimulated. Epinephrine increases our heart rate, stands our hair on end, constricts our pupils and superficial blood vessels, tightens our sphincter muscles. This brave defender of our physical status quo readies us for imagined or real battle. Other hormones coming from the adrenal medulla have the opposite effect during stress: the coward plays dead.

Physical responses are enhanced during stress. If the stress pathway is utilized often enough and conscious awareness of stress is lost, the conscious mind will perceive the heart's palpitation or the gut growling as illness.

Using internal imagery to master a dilemma promotes an understanding of the mechanisms of mind over body. A good example of this is breath-holding. Physiologically, when an individual is stressed, the pulse races. The act of breath-holding stimulates the vagus nerve and slows the heart rate and our breathing. We are not consciously aware that we are holding our breath, but that is what we are doing. If you can use visual imagery in this situation with positive results, you may be able to tackle more complex internal issues with imagery. Try it. Instead of breath-holding, you could visualize a dam, holding back raging waters (the racing pulse) to slow your heart rate in times of stress.

Using internal imagery during times of stress decreases the negative effects our physical and psychological conflicts have upon us. We are able to provide harmony to both our minds and our bodies during times of physical or mental stress.

Self-Confidence

Having trust in ourselves and our abilities is the ongoing re-sult of positive interactions in our social strata: work, church, home, school. If, in the process of maturing, an event occurred in which we received negative feedback about our performance, it will affect our future trust in our ability to function in a similar circumstance. At times, the negative reinforcement can become generalized and be applied to all tasks of a similar nature. Then, we get stuck in the need to do all tasks, perfectly, or not at all.

Perfectionism is the expectation that our pursuits in life should be goal directed to doing it all flawlessly. Perfectionism inhibits the learning curve of trial and error. If we honor the idea that faultless results should be the product of our endeavors, we may then become afraid to act, in fear that we will reveal our shameful imperfections. If the goal rests solely on flawless results, the road traveled to get there becomes irrelevant. Embarrassment and humiliation at making the wrong turn might be the award awaiting the perpetrator of a flawed experiment. This could stifle originality.

We must give up the perfectionist's expectations and learn to trust our perceptions, so that when acting upon them, we will be capable of analyzing the result and if we fail, we will have the courage to venture forward to try the task anew.

Accessing the Silent Stranger's visual imagery will teach us to trust our perceptions. Confronting our inner-critic and setting it aside will allow us to trust a basic, imaginative inner-self that accepts mistakes and doesn't hide from them, doesn't feel deprecated by failure, and uses any and all experiences as motivation for exploring new avenues of expression.

John, one of our subjects, was unhappy in his career choice of woodworking. The economy had taken a downturn and his managerial skills could not be sustained in a downsized economy. He felt he was a procrastinator and functioned at his best under the demands of production work. He undertook the exercises after endless nagging. He related an adversity to participating by stating, "I have nothing in common with artists. I don't have even a glimmer of the artistic nature." He stroked out a dark, ominous figure and a screaming face.

After learning the basic techniques, John frowned and scowled as he rubbed darks and lights on the paper. To his amazement, he produced an image of an owl. He did not recognize the owl until he stood up and stepped away from the drawing. It came from within.

His thought was, *"How odd that it really looks like an owl. Maybe I'm not as unartistic as I believe myself to be. And, I wasn't ashamed when I expressed my fears."* (Illustration #13)

John accepted the revelation of his inner artistry by combining his woodworking skills, his love of wood's expressive grain and his Silent Stranger to begin a new career sculpting humidors that are works of art.

Like John, you must perceive yourself in a constant state of achieving and you must trust yourself above all others.

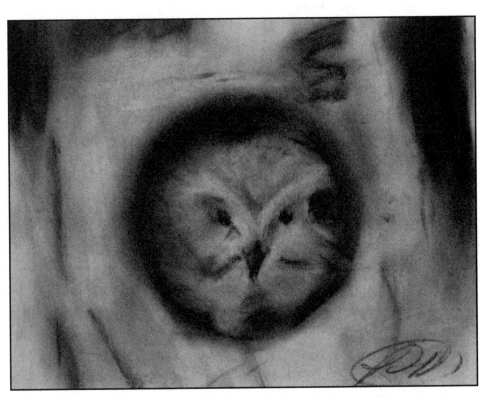

John's Hidden Owl
(Illustration 13)

Empowerment

One of our subjects, A.D., has visualized and drawn his ideal woman. Previously shy and inhibited, he has learned to express his fantasies and visions with charcoal and oil.

By using visual imagery and drawing out your feelings in your creations, the Silent Stranger will become known to you as the creative part of your being. You will rediscover the missing part of yourself that allows you the freedom to explore and anticipate without concern for the ramifications of the rigid, judging adult concept of self. You will become empowered to manifest tangible products of an open mind.

You will become a willing participant in matters of the heart: a passionate individual experiencing pleasure and going with the flow. You will take control, create order, and focus on your desires because you will be the creator. You will perceive and act on visions that are your own reality. You will trust that you are a capable administrator.

Concerns of the ego, the inner-critic, and other authoritative figures will become minimized. This will allow you to get on with the business of creating your own agenda for life! You can decide where the boundaries in which you choose to function, begin and end. You will be able to decide if you wish, to venture beyond those boundaries. You will be the only one setting your limits. You will control the source of your illumination.

You will determine your goals and estimate how boldly you wish to pursue them. You will be more in touch with how things affect you, and therefore, more able to estimate what you really want, based on how you really feel.

You will be confident in your ability to react appropriately. Your path becomes an adventure and you are up to the challenge! You will be more vigorous, able to express yourself with more abandon and able to tap into a source of mental energy not previously available.

By personally signing your impression you will have produced a product. You will have developed faith in your innate wisdom and trust in yourself as a creator. You will be empowered by your experience with the Silent Stranger, with a sense of freedom and an enhanced sense of gratification of your own creativity!

Passion

Creativity occurs as an outlet for the expression of two motivations: that of needing or wanting something (a solution, product, goal, means of expression), and that of pure, passionate inspiration. Passion is the exclamation point at the end of each innovative discovery or adventure.

Passion is a state of desire, a quest for blending with a feeling or need. It is all encompassing at the time it is experienced. Yet, the ability to flow with a passionate quest is frequently muted by an internal buffer, that ever present inner-critic.

An avid horsewoman related an experience that encompassed the concept of passion in an unusual way. She had worked hard to train one of her horses for exhibition. The horse was a beautiful creature but abjectly stubborn and subversive. She damned the horse and thought about the humiliation she was going to experience in the show ring. She developed endless schooling tricks to train the horse to have a proper ringside demeanor, but the horse had her number and was able to defeat the gimmicks she developed to settle his head, or slow his rapid gait.

One day, she got on his back with the thought that she loved the horse's spirit. She left him alone and enjoyed the feeling of his movement. She quit intellectualizing about the horse's performance and enjoyed the ride from the horse's point of view. Suddenly, she felt something different. The horse's head dropped to a show angle, his gait became slow and deliberate. She felt an intense pleasure as she became one with the horse. She visualized the horse's movement and the horse responded with the proper maneuver. She described the experience with awe, relating that it was one of the most moving, passionate encounters she had ever experienced. The horse won his class at the Pomona Fair and other riders actually took their hats off to honor "his Cadillac performance" as he received first place.

There is a sensual component to both creativity and passion. Creative expression is boundless when accompanied by passion. This passion can be enhanced by tactile stimulus, such as stroking with charcoal. Sensuality is a preoccupation with the bodily senses, rather than the intellect. Therefore, in the process of momentarily bypassing the intellect, visual imagery and creative expression are enhanced. The result is freedom without mental judgment.

Tactile pleasure is tantamount in the pursuit of rendering impressions. Senses are heightened, the ability to focus is increased, and to our delight and enjoyment, the emergence of a passionate self comes forth. Nothing can compare to total immersion in our perceptions and the passion we feel expressing and creating them.

Passion can be spontaneous. It may result in a sense of excitement, stimulation and heightened energy. A new and vigorous interest in things that were not previously seen may arouse an inordinate sensation. The question, "What if?" may lead to, "How could I? How could I have ever lived without these intense reactions to my new perceptions? How could I ever have responded in this life with anything less than this wonderful passion?"

There is a powerful role played by visual imagination in sexual passion and enhancement. Realizing that we are vulnerable to our base desire, the inner-critic may be incited to act as our censor, editing our concepts of sexuality and sensuality based on society's inhibitions about the subject.

The moment of passionate and highly sensual intimacy was

often expressed in Japanese prints by the curling of the toes. Expressing yourself through the tactile senses may be compared to lovemaking. The contact of the extremities with a texture that incites arousal is required to experience sensory pleasure. You delight in the experience of touching, your toes curl with the sensation. You are engaged in stimulating foreplay. You gently feel out and explore your subject. You touch and look at various parts, discovering previously unrecognized delights. You examine forbidden sights and enjoy the explosion of arousal. Your ordinary state of being is altered. You experience textures, hair, skin, as new delights. You gently, delicately, and at times roughly, allow your fingertips to graze the surface. You take great pleasure in recording how one form comes in contact with another.

You look at something intently and the experience of sight incites a physical sensation of desire. The concentration of energy as you focus makes you tingle with excitement. Your natural instincts as a voyeur are activated. And your inner-critic is screaming, *"Don't look! Don't stare!"* But the creation of imagery is essential, to go beyond the tactile toward passion and achieve, ultimately, ecstasy.

Passion leading to ecstasy is one of our highest aspirations. It provides a way for us to leave our physical bodies and become one with the universe. At the point of ecstasy we have no boundaries, we are infinite.

Attaining this passion and ecstasy should be the goal of all creative pursuit. But, taking abject pleasure in the physical senses is often limited by the restrictions of the inner-critic. The denial of passion appeases it. The individual seeks relief from its arguments instead of pursuing a creative and passionate experience. Passion is the ultimate form of expression. Silencing the inner-critic, is the gift the Silent Stranger gives you to truly experience emotion at its highest intensity, as ecstasy.

Intuition

Having a sense about things is the quality of being intuitive. Intuition springs from an inner knowledge, a "sixth sense." Sensing danger before it happens is intuitive. Perceiving harm before it has been inflicted has been reported. Arguments abound related to the genetic, environmental, sociologic or the psychological origins of this innate knowledge. Whatever its origin, intuition is a powerful tool.

When Lidia was living in Cuba, just prior to Castro's take over, there was marked social unrest. Certain households were targeted by one faction or another to be attacked. One night she was at home with her young auntie. She was sitting in the living room on a rocking chair while her auntie was preparing to retire in the front bedroom. Lidia had an uncanny feeling that someone was watching her and because of that feeling, she didn't retire to her room at the back of the main house. Suddenly there was a loud blast. Someone had thrown a pipe bomb that exploded towards the rear of the house near her room.

❖   ❖   ❖

The confidence to commit to an inner awareness and act upon it is an intuitive quality. Rationalizing (there's that nasty critic again!) can inhibit the capacity to react spontaneously to an unknown factor and can block the ability to be intuitive. Finding an image in charcoal strokes of darks and lights is an intuitive process. It entails having the confidence to trust an inner-knowledge to 'go with it' rather than acting on the intellectual need to carry out a predefined plan.

Acting on intuition excites the Silent Stranger. The Stranger's intuitive capabilities come from the ability to trust a 'sense' as readily as a fact. Our Stranger can expedite our ability to react intuitively by magnifying that sense with visual projections of, 'what ifs.'

The projections occur rapidly, delivering different scenarios from our mental landscape faster than our intellect can process the data. You might find a satisfying sense of composition and a wealth of hidden implications that are intuitively correct by acting on the Stranger's 'what-ifs.'

An intuitive person can be common-sensical in problem solving, but imaginative in anticipating the road blocks that will be met on the path to solving a problem. The Stranger can soar to unimagined heights by enhancing our intuitive nature.

Imagination and Inner Visions

The talent of our imagination is its capacity to form inner-imagery from mental associations. Imagination is the nidus of creative endeavor. Fantasy is the handmaiden of imagination, but acts as a superficial servant to it. Fantasy is frisky and playful. Imagination is ponderous and ardent in its goals.

The ability to be imaginative is present in each of us. But the aptitude to create from imaginative reverie, initially an innate skill, might have been lost in the process of maturing. Expressing imagination can involve the burden of embarrassment or humiliation. The block that tries to avoid possible dishonor is our ever present inner-critic.

When the overt expression of our imagination has been blocked, positive reinforcement is needed to once again, permit its outward expression. This positive reinforcement allows us to express outwardly, concepts from our inner world, and will lead to the capacity to express the fertile seeds of our imagination.

Inner visions, in a healthy adult, are the core of imagination and fantasy. What inspires these panoramic visions is unknown. Perhaps they are merely a physiologic display of a spontaneous discharge from a mental storage bank, or simply the rods and cones of our eyes, which the brain organizes into a whole image? They can certainly be beautiful images. The need to express them can be fulfilled, because the visual language of the Silent Stranger is the pathway to a better view of the mental fireworks!

There is no mystery after knowledge becomes absolute. But the acquisition of knowledge, the solving of the mystery, is a great adventure. To understand the abstract concepts of creativity, imagination, fantasy, passion and inner vision is a lifetime endeavor. So is self-understanding. Since you are the only living witness to all of your life events, you are your own greatest mystery. Only you can chronicle your life passages and experience your individuality in its' fullest potential.

CHAPTER SIX

Further Information About Your Silent Stranger

As you draw on your Silent Stranger's power, you will find the keys to self-acceptance and self-fulfillment.

The Heart of the Matter

The power of self expression leads to inspiration...

the heart of the matter...

The pulsing flow to a creative life.

And creativity was the beginning of it all

as life bled from the Creator's touch

to give us "heart"

a beat strong within...

free to pulse at its own pace.

It is the fiber of our uniqueness

contracting and expanding...

without which

all is arrested...

—LIDIA'S CONCEPT
OF CREATIVITY

＊　＊　＊

THE HEART OF THE MATTER is that each of us has been given a life to lead. That life should be a celebration of our individuality, not a suppression of it. It should be lived with freedom and choice.

The heart of the matter is that the Stranger inspires the mind to experience perceptions that are based on individual experience. The Silent Stranger, once freed, will go about the business of expressing the truest impression of the our personality.

One who engages in the search for the Silent Stranger opens the path to new opportunities and new possibilities.

＊　＊　＊

Esoterica
Or... Now That You're Initiated

There is No Playful Inner Child!

Now that you understand the Silent Stranger and the psychology of the inner-critic you will see that, in your future readings on self-improvement, you will be one step ahead when discussions center around the psyche and the inner child.

There are a multitude of books written and seminars given on healing the 'wounded inner child.' HOMECOMING by John Bradshaw, finds fault with every mechanism society has in place to socialize the child/adult: the unknowingly wounded and wounding parents; the judgmental school system; the punitive church. Bradshaw's concept about self-acceptance is valid, but his premise is wrong. Reclaiming the wounded inner child that requires detoxification and healing is irrelevant. There might possibly be a battle-scarred adult. In the process of joining the regiment of society, the maturing soldier might have been the scapegoat or the target during warfare, but those experiences have now made that person a worthy warrior. Otherwise, we may as well pull the covers over our heads and stay in bed with our thoughts about how we were victimized and how we should have been raised! We should be cocooned away from all the negatives life has to offer.

In a similar vein, the perpetually evolving adult can be inhibited by internalized negatives. Dr. Pauline Rose Clance, in THE IMPOSTOR PHENOMENON, establishes a valid case for the destructive potential of the inner-critic. The 'IP' phenomenon relates to an achiever's inability to accept their success, *"It wasn't me. I was just at the right place at the right time,"* or *"I just worked harder,"* or *"I just studied harder."* According to Dr. Clance, one aspect of this inability to accept the accolades due for one's success is the role the family unit relegated to the sufferer. Her suggestions to overcome the mask of martyr and enjoy the accolades is, *"...try to remember what you actually thought at the time, and write down that mental response."* Obviously, the rational mind of the maturing individual took up the banner, *"I'm not good enough."* Dr. Clance expounds further with the idea that the impostor phenomenon stems from a fear of feeling foolish, embarrassed or shamed. Oh, what a bad, bad inner-critic! But, if we identify with this syndrome, we're already ahead because we've learned how to set the bad critic aside.

Take up the gauntlet and challenge yourself to silence your critic and reclaim your stranger. Meld the stranger's potent source of visual imagery with your current fund of knowledge—including all the joy and pain that inspired your learning. Don't waste time blaming the past that precipitated your present state, but take up all the tools you've acquired to date and utilize them to create a rewarding future.

The deeper the pain of growing, the greater the capacity to generate a life plan that will be free of those encumbrances. Make the adult the playful entrant into life's battles instead of assigning this task to the 'inner child.' Playtime should be based on liberating the adult that exists at this time, not a vulnerable child that you've retrieved from the past. Playing is a participation in an imaginative or fanciful endeavor. Giving outward expression to a need for movement or to express ideas with childish abandon tempered by maturity is an exhilarating experience. You need your current fund of knowledge to move forward with this new concept of creativity. And...you certainly do not want to repeat the process of growing up!

Self-Validation is Not Self-Centered

To validate oneself removes the need for validation from others. It's a liberating experience. The passage into the world of self-validation requires acting on faith and meeting your Silent Stranger which enables you to acquire an understanding of the true beauty that exists in the visual imagery of your inner-self. Experiencing this imagery permits a knowledge of your own innate creativity and goodness. Your self-worth will be understood by the most important persons: Me, myself and I!

The need for validation will no longer come from others. Anything that comes your way in your relationships is an embellishment, because you are complete unto yourself. As you learn to trust and accept yourself, you also learn to accept others as they are.

Self-Improvement Propaganda Can Be Cultish

Yes it can, unless you are able to take the seed and nurture it on your own. Your journey of self-discovery should not be based on someone else's dictates. Your life history is an individual event. If you are vegetating, stunted with boredom, the remedy to what ails you is not a collective experience. There is no generic fertilizer to cure all your ills. You now have the Silent Stranger, the tools and the fertile soil to nurture a unique sense of self worth. Use the tools, sow your own seeds and cultivate your own garden!

❂   ❂   ❂

The June gloom was sitting at the horizon, a passive mass, just waiting. The precipitation crept inland each night. Where it hung heavily, sounds echoed. Dinosaurs and the end of the world were a possibility, enveloped and hidden in the mist along the coastline of San Diego.

Influenced by the eerie heaviness in the evening air, things not readily seen preoccupied our thoughts as we sat on the terrace that overlooked the hills. Not long ago, the Heaven's Gate cult had committed mass suicide in the nearby community of Rancho Santa Fe.

"Why do people give up their spirits so readily to someone else's concept of reality?" Hyacinthe said, puzzled by the mass mentality of the cult.

"I've come face to face with that aspect of human nature," I replied. "When I was in training, during my year as an intern, I had the most enthusiastic medical student under me. He was constantly dogging my heels, participating in every little nuance of each case. I adored his tenacity. In my estimation, he was going to be a wonderful doctor. He ended up being the physician for the Jonestown cult and mixed the fatal Kool-Aid potion."

Hyacinthe expressed her shock loudly, over the howling and yelping of the coyotes that were echoing out of the misty night.

"It's true," I continued. "But the issue in my mind at the time was how such a caring, intelligent person could have committed such an act. It seemed to me that his belief system was completely vulnerable to a need to belong, to be accepted. We found out that the People's Temple had actually put him through medical school. His excellent performance during training, was based on his all encompassing need for acceptance, even mine."

The coyotes yelped madly. The yelps blended into a wild cacophony of frenetic, primitive screeching that was chilling in its ferocity.

"It still doesn't explain why he gave up his belief system to a cult," Hyacinthe said as she challenged me to come up with a better explanation.

I didn't have an appropriate explanation, other than to answer that he probably had no self-worth or imagination, and he had relied on others to give it to him. Unfortunately, he picked the wrong group of others.

❖   ❖   ❖

The work required to feel fulfillment and self-knowledge is not free. It requires introspection and a capacity to put your paddles in the water, no matter where the current is propelling you, and to guide your own canoe. You own that canoe. It won't do you any good to curse the inadequacies of the canoe maker as you fight the raging current.

Since each of us is a very individual collection of experiences, no one else can enter your diary and cement a gold star of self-worth and approval there. Only you can. Your life experiences belong to you and to no one else. Take the tools that work for you and apply them to your individuality instead of becoming a follower of another's theories about what is good for you. Learn to make your own mark.

Sharing Your Discovery

In Exercise 10 you experienced the concept of "See One, Do One, Teach One." As you progress beyond the rigid methods of expression previously known to you, as you really learn to see, and to trust in the capacity to flow with visual imagery, you can become a teacher.

Your participation in the exercises was your preparation to educate others. The quality with which you share your experience rests with the knowledge of several factors:

I. **Acknowledge** the nonlinear concept of visual imagery. It is a manifestation of past experiences of an intelligent, functional adult and it will manifest itself.

Lidia was taunted by one of our subjects to draw her impression of a gaudy tattoo of a wolf. It took her seconds to realize the end result. An inner awareness compelled her to place her drawing on the diagonal which implied something sinister, and then to swipe through it with the eraser to imply movement. (Illustration #14)

2. **Believe** that there is an inner-critic that will attempt to block this method of creative expression.

> One of our subjects, L.S., was doing the doing the exercises. She had received no explanation about the concept of the inner-critic. While doing the exercise on anger, she muttered loudly to herself when she thought we were out of earshot, "Oh, I'm not that angry," after she had smeared two bold lines on the paper. "If I put a circle around it, Lidia and Hyacinthe won't know how explosive I am." Her inner-critic was actively attempting to block what she felt was a character flaw. (Illustration #15)

3. **Understand** the ability to hear, and then quiet the inner-critic. This is essential to manifest visual imagery.

> J. H. was doing the exercise on fear. He related that his inner-critic cautioned him that if he expressed his fear he would become vulnerable. This concerned him. After further exercises, he went back and changed an austere black landscape to a sinister hooded figure. He finally told us that the hooded figure was the true inner landscape of his fear. (Illustration #16)

4. **Know** that there is a Silent Stranger, and that anyone can access it. Draw on your own experience to realize this concept, or... you can take a look at Lidia's first drawing.

5. **Trust** yourself and really see beyond the obvious. Refresh your memory on this point by looking back to the story of the homeless man under the tree.

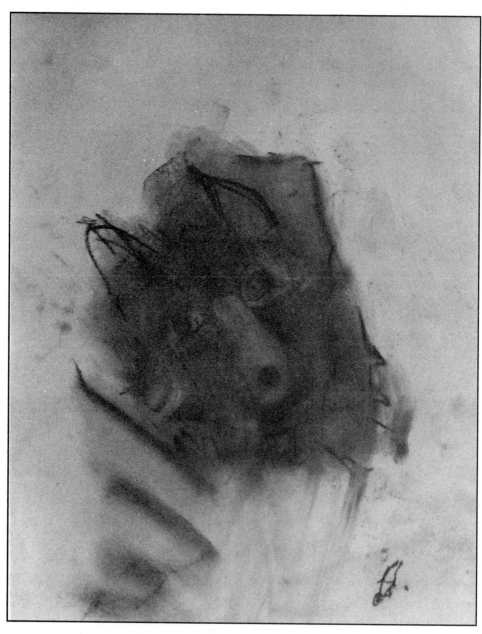

The Two-Second Wolf
(Illustration #14)

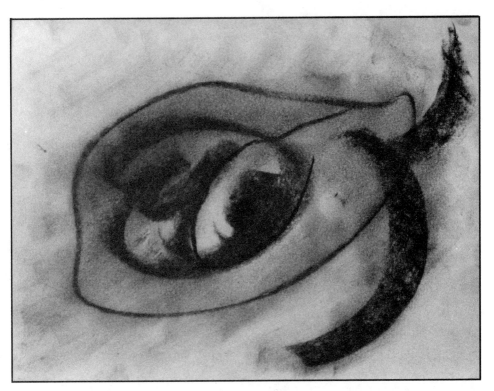

The Angry Avocado
(Illustration #15)

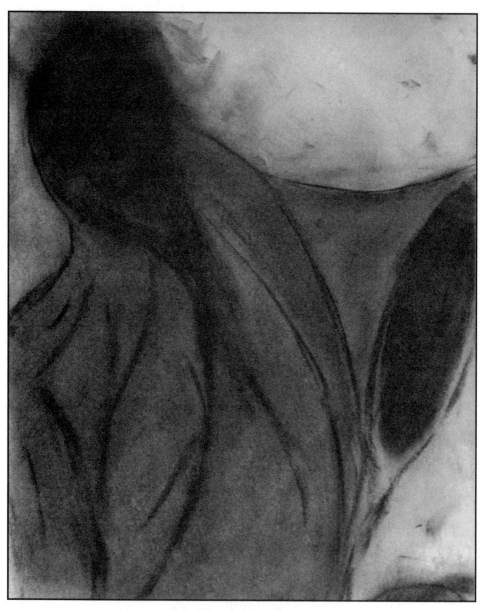

The Hooded Landscape
(Illustration #16)

The Psychology of the Silent Stranger

The Silent Stranger relates to the psychology of the functional (mentally healthy) individual. Psychosis and severe neurosis are not a part of the Stranger's realm in the context of this book. Theories on mental illness abound and are as numerous as the different schools of psychotherapy.

Freudian psychology analyzes individual motivation and behavior based on components of the personality that include the unconscious, the subconscious and the conscious. This school is the basis of classical psychoanalysis. In the example of the patient with panic attacks in Chapter Two, Freudian theory would suggest that an unconscious, repressed conflict is the basis for the patient's physical symptoms. The psychoanalytical technique would tend to view the patient's concept of what is wrong as 'irrelevant.' The patient cannot reason his way out of the pickle he is in because his awareness is superficial to his inner mechanisms. The patient's conscious explanation of remembering the time he almost drowned would probably be considered a rationalization. What he really needs is couch time, free association, and regression so that the therapist can figure out how to fix what is broken.

Strict behaviorists on the other hand, use a similar technique to reject an individual's reflections in his attempt to understand his behavior. Only a behavior that can be observed by the clinician is relevant to solving the puzzle. The saying, "If a tree fell in a forest and nobody saw it..." illuminates the behaviorists approach, 'if it's not witnessed, it never happened.'

Organic psychotherapy, a newer branch of psychiatric medicine, treats our body with chemicals. The theory is that chemicals within the brain are causing a disturbance. The outward symptoms are a manifestation of an underlying imbalance of these chemicals. Our panic attack patient would be given medication to treat the anxiety. This pharmacological approach has been quite successful in treating depression and other mental disorders. The medication replenishes neurotransmitters that are depleted in the emotional control center of the brain. Better living through modern chemistry!

Cognitive therapists do recognize individual conscious ideation and the significance of the individual's subliminal voice. Aaron Beck in his book, COGNITIVE THERAPY AND THE EMOTIONAL DISORDERS, states, "In the course of development, his awareness of his own psychological experiences crystallizes into defined self-observations, which eventually expand into generalizations." The cognitive approach would teach the panic attack patient to recognize the inner-critic. Cognitive therapists avoid delving deep into repressed memories, believing that the individual is capable of participating in their care by becoming an observer and interpreter of his or her 'inner-reality.' The approach, with respect to the inner psyche, is, "If it's not broken, don't fix it."

The common word related to these schools of thought is, 'individual.' Although each school of psychotherapy deals with the individual, they all have different concepts of 'self.' No one set of psychological rules, or school of thought can explain the 'individual' because each individual's world is a unique and personal experience.

THE SILENT STRANGER IS NOT:

- The Freudian equivalent of the Id.[1]

- The suppressed inner child.

- The toxic by-product of bad parenting.

- The moderator of an individual's overt behavior.

THE SILENT STRANGER IS:

- The birth place of visual imagery and the world of 'what-ifs.'

- The moderator of the rational mind.

- A melding of the mature adult with the imaginative child.

- That part of ourselves we lost contact with long ago and sorely miss.

- The altruistic being of self-acceptance and unconditional love.

The Silent Stranger is our common thread of individuality, because the Silent Stranger is...all of us, individually and collectively as the following chapter will help demonstrate.

---

1. In Freudian psychology there are three components to personality: the id (the primitive impulses), the ego (the concept of self), and the superego (internalized mores).

CHAPTER SEVEN

≈

A Few Case Studies

A Vision

Amid white cloud formations
a visionary stallion may appear.
How can it fly on wings of fear?

Wind caresses the stallion ride.
Dreams are borne on clouds of air.
Love so bound by human pride
will fly on wings of ecstasy.

The world is filled with stallion's delight.
Illumined in the cells with care.
Radiance is divine and within your sight
is the whiteness of an angel's hair.

See a unicorn, symbol of peace.
See a Pegasus amid the gleam.
Enchanted visions never cease.
Nothing is what it may seem.

In such a vision are many things.
Two parts of the world join as one.
A hummingbird, though it may not sing,
still knows when dreams are done.

—HYACINTHE

Case Studies

*T*he subjects who participated in our study came from a wide range of educational and professional backgrounds. New art students, friends and co-workers participated. We chose not to include Hyacinthe's private art students because their drawing techniques were established which would make validation of the theory difficult without some loss of objectivity.

The tactile impact of the techniques was validated by Hyacinthe's volunteer work at the San Diego Center for the Blind. The concept of the inner-critic and the facilitated pathway went from hypothetical to theoretical as each of our subjects verified a common experience by seeking the Stranger without the investigator's input. The exercises evolved by matching expected goals to those experienced by the subjects.

We would like to share some of their experiences with you:

CASE ONE: A. D.

Al, a sixty-one year-old engineer, was born in Massachusetts. He had wanted to take art lessons with Hyacinthe for three years. He told us how it was to grow up in a reserved family where emotions were not expressed. Al shared with us that he had low self-esteem and an alienating sense of deep loneliness. He had explored the four corners of the earth in search of 'something' that would fill the void he experienced. His quest included guru searching in India, and living in an ashram. He meditated, read countless books and discovered something very important, "I didn't know anything about myself." He found his work unfulfilling, and went into early semi-retirement.

Al discovered the missing part of himself when he decided to try another path in his search for self. He touched charcoal to paper, expressed himself, and never went back to his previous rigid manner of expression.

He learned drawing from scratch and found expressing visual imagery to be a transforming experience. As he developed skills with charcoal, he discovered meaningful images in his drawings. He found that he was also developing a new perspective about life. His self-esteem sky-rocketed. He found relief from stress. He related the most important lesson matter-of-factly: "I learned to change things by changing myself."

A provoking encounter with his Silent Stranger occurred when he was asked to make two drawings at once. He chose as his subject a woman. One woman was an old, somber, hooded crone. The defining lines for this drawing were rigid. The other drawing was of a woman arched over the background image of the crone. Her form was soft and curving with few lines needed to define her femininity. She was removing her undergarments! No one was more surprised than Al. (Illustrations #17 and #18)

His new perspective overwhelmed him with a need to give something back and he commenced doing volunteer work at the San Diego Center for the Blind. Within a few months the skies opened up. After sending out his first resume, he found a rewarding job in engineering that allowed him to express his creativity.

Several years before, Al had undergone a hip replacement. He had lost coordination and physical strength in his lower extremities. He felt that expressing himself took attention away from his physical discomfort and helped him to heal.

Al is still battling with his inner-critic. When asked about his art, he discusses it rigidly with his arms crossed defensively in front

(After Rembrandt)

Rembrandt's Crone
(Illustration #17)

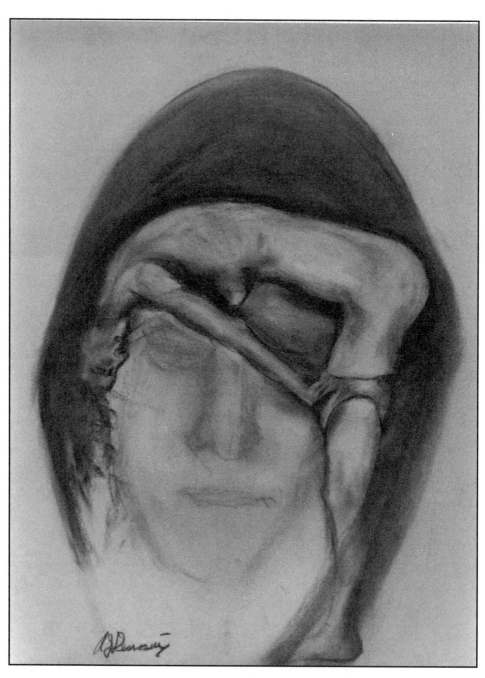

The Other Woman
(Illustration #18)

of him. Even his smile is rigid and of short duration. When we switch to the subject of his Silent Stranger, Al's entire demeanor changes. He conveys power and confidence. His arms move about as he uses body language to emphasize his words. They are flowing, graceful movements. He says that with his Silent Stranger he feels physically transformed and whole. (Illustration #19)

CASE TWO: J. R. H.

John, a forty-two year-old production manager, disdained art and men who expressed their feminine side. He was guarded in all his relationships because he didn't want to feel vulnerable. He defined himself as a "chronic procrastinator...except at work."

He was a reluctant subject who felt the request to stroke charcoal on paper was absolutely ridiculous. He focused on the silliness of our requests to express anger and fear with his fingers. In an attempt to keep the lesson silly, he stroked out a female breast, but an inner need changed the image to a screaming face. This shocked and embarrassed him. He quickly tried to regain control by stating that the rendition was an "orgasmic woman." (Illustration #20)

After several sessions, John developed a keen awareness of the block that had been imposed on his earlier sessions by his fear of being shamed or embarrassed. He began to relax and express himself. With his new perspective he developed a sensitivity about the feelings of others. He had a son from a previous marriage. A new intuitive sense that something was wrong with his son's home environment developed. This lead to the discovery that the child's mother was being physically abused. John was able to maintain a supportive role towards his ex-wife while he assumed the role of primary caretaker for his son.

After doing the exercises, John felt a need to communicate on a deeper level and sought a spiritual meaning to his daily life.

Al and His Silent Stranger
(Illustration #19)

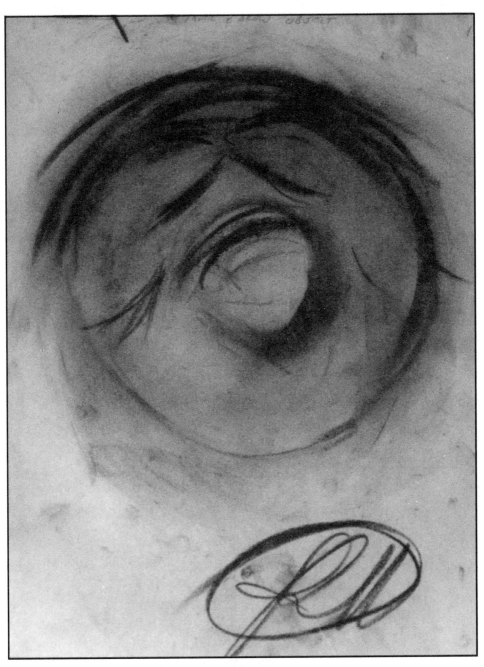

The Screaming Breast
(Illustration #20)

He attended several retreats and felt open and trusting enough to express himself without fear of embarrassing ramifications. He found he was able to converse about sensitive issues without his buttons being pushed. He claimed that he would not have been open to the ideas presented at the retreats if he had not done the exercises.

CASE THREE: L. S.

L. S. is a thirty-seven year-old gentlewoman of Hispanic origin who is employed as a certified medical assistant. She undertook the exercises feeling a guarded curiosity for the subject matter. She did not feel that she was artistic. She felt frustrated in that she couldn't see what she wanted to see. She was extremely uptight, but wouldn't quit. When she finally decided to play, rather than force the issue, she felt herself beginning to relax and enjoy smearing the charcoal. A woman in a fetal position materialized for her.

After smearing this imagery, she told us she experienced feelings from her past when her family was divided. Her mother and father were living in the United States, while she and her older siblings were living in Mexico. She felt that images related to these issues were present in her smears.

The amusing aspect of her experience was her husband's reaction. She giggled as she related his chagrin. "What do you think you are doing?" he asked, looking at the charcoal smeared table. "Are you prepared to buy a new table and paint the walls?"

"It washes off," she responded as she continued working.

Her husband went off to nap for awhile and returned. "Are you still at it? Just look at the table! It's completely black! How are you ever going to get it clean?"

The only way she could stop his criticism was to invite him to join her. He chose to remain absent until she was finished.

She chuckled as she commented that she really wanted him to get dirty, but the threat to him was a side benefit for her. She enjoyed smearing and looking for images well into the night... by herself, without her 'external' inner-critic. (Illustration #21)

CASE FOUR: P. H.

Philip is a fifty-four year-old retired medical social worker. He is legally blind secondary to a condition known as retinitis pigmentosa. Because of his medical condition, he had never attempted to draw and he had certainly never considered himself artistic.

He remembers having poor eyesight until 1983. Light perception persisted until 1986. He lost all vision in 1987.

He related having feelings of low self-esteem in his working environment where he functioned as a social worker in Child Protective Services. He felt his work was viewed skeptically and in a condescending manner because of his physical handicap.

He told us that he occasionally thought he still saw things. For example, he could walk along a sidewalk edge and see grass, but when he stopped and concentrated, he realized that he was only imagining what he was 'seeing.'

As part of a group at The San Diego Institute for the Blind, Philip decided to try drawing. For several months, he ruminated, *"Why should I waste my time? I can't see."* Conceding to participate made him feel foolish.

When he finally sat down to express himself on paper he felt silly, tense and childish. Smearing on paper reminded him of finger-painting. He thought somebody was going to look at his smearing and think it was infantile. He gradually relaxed with the exercises, and eventually felt like he was returning to an earlier age when his life was less stressful. One day he realized he was having a really good time!

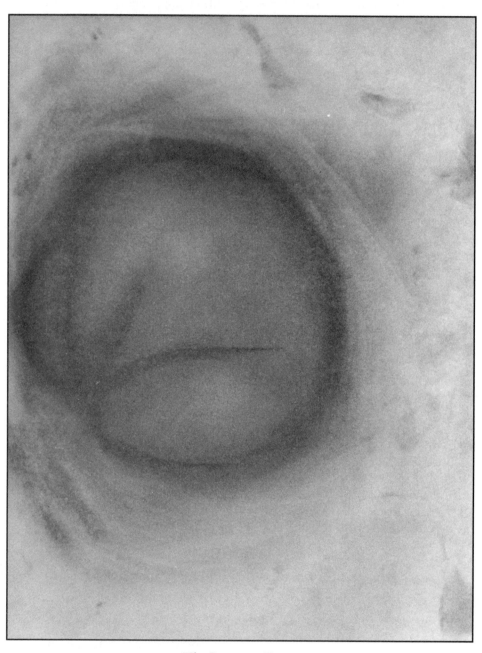

The Pregnant Fetus

(Illustration #21)

Philip gained confidence by drawing, but when praised by Hyacinthe he felt she probably said that to everyone. He felt the praise was given because he was blind. Then one day his work was hung on a wall and he heard other people praise it!

He subsequently tried to express a feeling through his art. He was unsure of the end result since he couldn't see it, but felt content that he had at least tried to express himself.

He gained great insight when he tried to depict, on paper, visual images that had been flashing across his mind. He told us of seeing 'flickering' faces that moved rapidly across his mental landscape. He could not understand the source of the imagery. Because he had been visually impaired since an early age, faces had never been a primary focus for him. He concentrated instead on mannerisms, a person's way of walking, their hair, but never their face since he couldn't really see the fine detail. He had explained his visions to his doctors who could only conclude that he was having 'delusions or hallucinations.'

Phillip explained that in order to draw these 'hallucinations,' he had to stop the projector because the visions never stood still. He had to work in a flash, because the visual picture changed before he could mentally evaluate it... "red dots flickered everywhere and were distracting."

Philip shared that his experience with his Silent Stranger made him aware of a voice that was blocking his expression and self-esteem. With his new awareness, he sought professional care and was able to reclaim his self-esteem. Learning to appreciate himself taught him greater compassion towards others.

He is now aware that he is capable of doing something creative with imagery even though he is blind. That feeling comforts him although he still lives with his constant 'flickering images.' Now, however, he is empowered to communicate these images. He sees without looking. (Illustration #22)

Philip's Flickering Face
(Illustration #22)

CASE FIVE: S. M.

Shawna is a twenty-six year-old woman, and a professional care-giver. Shawna undertook the exercises with great enthusiasm. She liked the idea of getting dirty, because one of her hobbies was furniture refinishing.

At first she felt tense when she began the exercises. A voice was telling her that she was not paying attention; that this was not supposed to be fun. The harder she tried to flow with the exercises, the louder her inner-critic became. She was adamant about 'shutting the voice up.' Then all at once she discovered two images that were very comparable to Case Three. (Illustrations #23A and #23B)

By the way... Shawna is a newly wed.

CASE SIX: P. B.

Pam is a thirty-three year-old registered nurse and a military officer. She is driven, a perfectionist at her duties as a division officer, but equally able to find humor in almost anything.

She did the exercise with a group of four subjects. Without a doubt, this woman had the loudest inner-critic we had ever heard!

When Pam sat down to smear her hands with charcoal, she assumed a very somber expression. There were loud sighs and copious, unintelligible mutterings. She seemed extremely tense... until she yelled at the upper limits of the scale of obnoxious sounds, "I am the creator and I sure am mad!" The rafters shook with the intensity of her shout!

Her first rendition depicted a human form enveloped and being chewed up by the evil inner-critic! She recognized the 'people-eater' in her smears when asked to review the material she had done.

Subsequent to her discovery, Pam related that she had quit drawing when she was nine years-old after her mother told her she

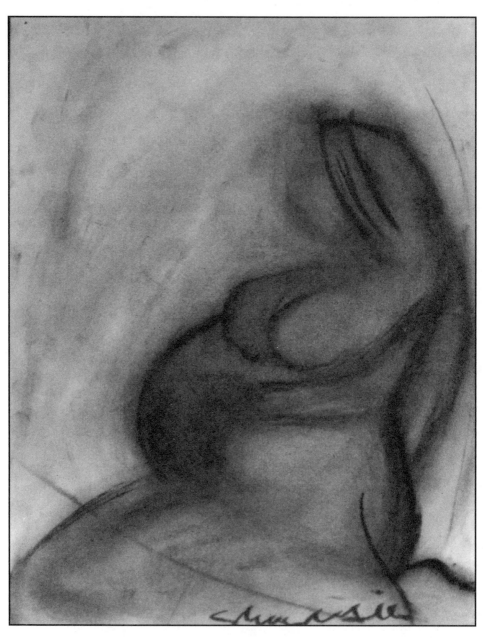

The Cowled Pregnancy
(Illustration #23A)

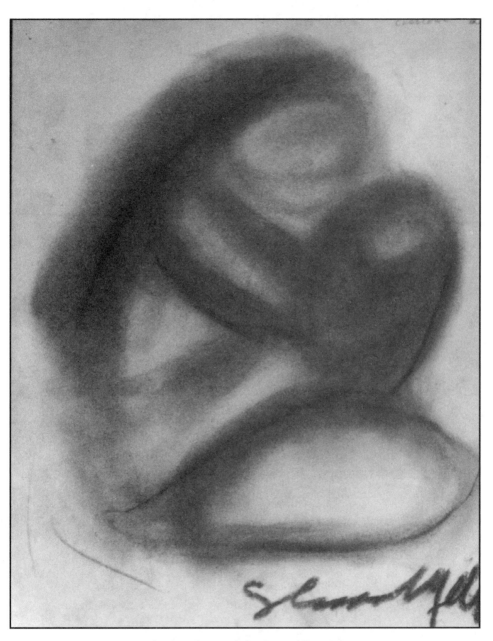

The Mother and the Potted Papoose
(Illustration #23B)

was too old for dolls and coloring. She remembered that her mother gathered all of her dolls and got rid of them. But she also recalled that drawing and doing things by herself was comforting when she was younger. She was a loner and felt wonderfully content with her dolls and drawing projects. She felt happy with her inanimate companions as her means of expression.

The night after she did the exercises, she told us she experienced a 'profound sleep.' She was exhausted and felt cleansed. (Illustration #24)

CASE SEVEN: D. P.

Donna is a fifty year-old licensed vocational nurse working in a civil service position. Her job entails maintaining the smooth functioning of the clinic she works in, as well as counseling patients for gastrorenterologic procedures and monitoring patients on blood thinners.

She undertook the exercises with a group of four other participants. She was noticeably quiet throughout her participation in the exercises. Donna said she felt challenged by a voice that repeatedly told her she didn't have any talent. She persisted, noting that she wanted to perform.

To execute the first cup she commanded herself, *"Just do it! Don't worry about it!"* and then she was able to relax. She knew that she was involved in a fascinating experience.

Later, when she looked at her work, Donna said she had been afraid. She was astonished when she found images in her random strokings. The images she had produced "from within" were expressed with the new tools she had acquired, her Silent Stranger. (Illustration #25)

CASE EIGHT: J. L.

Jacqueline works in retail. She is a divorced mother of three

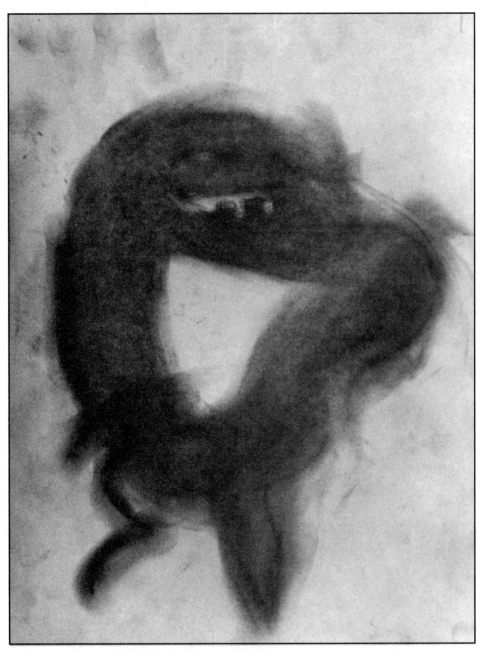

Endless Circle: The Man-Eating Inner-Critic
(Illustration #24)

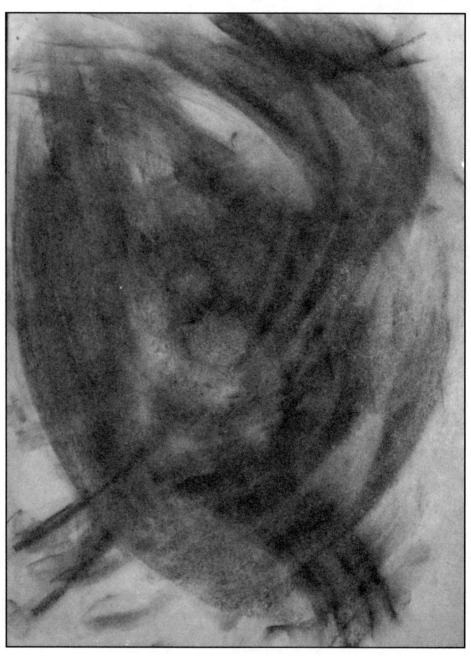

The Unrecognized Face
(Illustration #25)

grown daughters, including a set of twins. She has managed the modeling careers of her twin daughters who now have lives of their own. She sorely misses her granddaughter who lives with her mother in Italy.

She approached the exercises quite openly although she was amused at the idea of dirtying her hands. She explained, "After years of admonishing my girls not to get dirty, I worry that I was putting limitations on them in favor of a clean house."

Her first marks were playful renditions of fluffy, fantasy animals. (Illustration #26)

During a subsequent exercise she defined what appeared to be a large male organ dominating the profile of a figure. Even after the male organ was pointed out to her, she refused to recognize it. Her inner-critic was flabbergasted into abject denial.

Jacqueline had found a new sense of freedom and wished to pursue further creative areas of expression—with dirty fingers! (Illustration #27)

The didactic theory of the Silent Stranger was not shared with the subjects prior to their participation in the exercises. In all cases the subjects were asked, and they affirmed that they felt there was a part of themselves they were no longer in contact with. There was a sense that there was something hidden within them. As they did the exercises each subject related they became aware of an inner-critic presenting obstacles to free expression.

When they defied their inner-critic, they experienced a range of sensations from a sense of relaxation and enjoyment, to a sense of discovery and wonder.

Whether the subjects proceeded to perfect an artistic means of expression or found the knowledge with which to defy their inner-critic, most became aware that something simultaneously empowering and comforting had occurred. May you meet your Silent Stranger soon!

Monkey, Fish and Wormlike Creature
(Illustration #26)

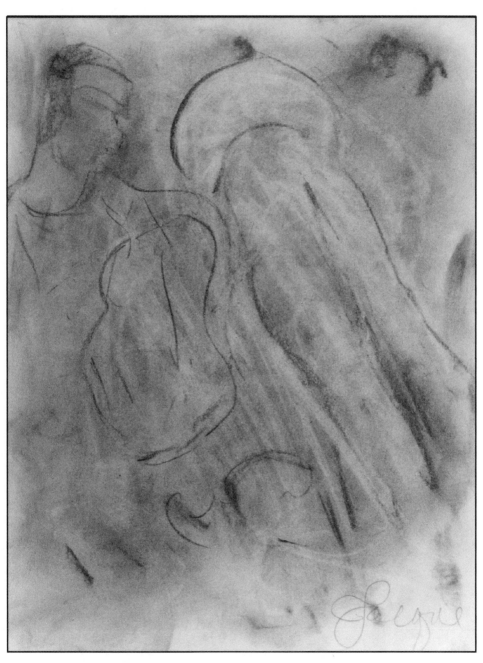

Male Organ and Musician
(Illustration #27)

EPILOGUE

. . . the Master said, "Once there lived a village of creatures along the bottom of a great crystal river.

The current of the river swept silently over them all— young and old, rich and poor, good and evil, the current going its own way, knowing only its own crystal self.

Each creature in its own manner clung tightly to the twigs and rocks of the river bottom, for clinging was their way of life, and resisting the current was what each had learned from birth.

. . . But one creature said at last, 'I am tired of clinging. Though I cannot see it with my eyes, I trust that the current knows where it is going. I shall let go, and let it take me where it will. Clinging, I shall die of boredom.'

. . . The other creatures laughed and said, 'Fool! Let go, and that current you worship will throw you tumbled and smashed across the rocks, and you will die quicker than boredom!'

. . . But the one heeded them not, and taking a breath did let go, and at once was tumbled and smashed by the current across the rocks.

. . . Yet in time, as the creature refused to cling again, the current lifted him free from the bottom, and he was bruised and hurt no more". . .

—ILLUSIONS: THE ADVENTURES OF A RELUCTANT MESSIAH BY RICHARD BACH

The Lessons Learned

Seeking. . . by looking into the brain (every creature has one), you cannot find the mind. Looking into the heart (a necessary organ but synthetic ones have been made), you cannot find the soul. Surgeons can attest to these facts. Scalpels at the ready, they are aware of the anatomy and physiology of their arena, but bewildered by the mystery of the 'I'ness of life. Geneticists can analyze DNA and RNA, the genetic codes of our beings. But Dolly, the cloned sheep, does not possess her mother's adult sheep wisdom nor the knowledge of her mother's life. She must live her existence from her own perspective. Looking at the person, as a whole or cell by cell, one does not find the center of their individuality. But, the mind, the soul, individuality still exist.

In researching and writing this book, we sought and found that the Silent Stranger, our Adult Creator, does exist. Looking at our own artistic smears we found an inner reality that is unique to each individual, but is inspired by an aspect of the psyche that is common to us all: the Silent Stranger.

Why Silent? Because speech is the basis of rationalization, the core of linear thought and expression, the incarcerating tool of the inner-critic. You cannot scream, rationalize or cajole the Stranger into wakefulness. Imagination is silent, visual and all encompassing. It is the Stranger's impetus. Imaginative reverie is the pathway. The Stranger approaches you along this path with the tools we have provided.

When you meet your Stranger, the introduction is sweet, a homecoming. You instinctively know that the essence of all your wishes, hopes and aspirations are within you.

As you become reacquainted with your Stranger you will find

lilac sheets, flying carpets, playgrounds, the mysteries at the end of the rainbow. Your Stranger will lift you high enough to see your entire world anew.

Some of our subjects approached their Silent Stranger with a great deal of hunger. When introduced, they grasped their Stranger's hand with an urgency and were reluctant to let go. These bonding reunions were present in individuals who wanted to experience life more intensely. They were willing to be lifted by the current and float freely into unknown territory with the Stranger. Our subjects who were forty years of age and older had excelled in their career goals, but felt a need to find a deeper meaning in their daily activities and life goals. There was an intensity in their search and a commitment to nurture their new relationship with the Silent Stranger.

Our younger subjects (twenty to thirty years of age) put their hands out in a "gimme a high-five, glad-to-meet ya" approach. They were more accepting and less inquisitive of the Stranger's appearance in their charcoal renderings. Their initial impressions were usually described as a tense feeling followed by a, 'this is fun' sensation. They generally related feeling either exhausted or very relaxed after participating in the exercises.

You can teach yourself to break bread with your Stranger anyway you choose. If the artistic wand of drawing proves worthy, continue to cast spells with it.

Use your creative soul to find your own way to stay in contact with your Stranger! The authors hope that anyone meeting their Adult Creator will travel on a life-path flourishing with self-acceptance, aiming towards a destination of empathy for others.

May your pathway be facilitated! May your inner-critic meet a detour!... May you find the expression of your creativity a worthy goal!

—Lidia Everett, M.D.

Seeking The See King (King of the Sea)

Once there was a child whose fathers' ancestors were of noble blood. The father was forced by the Great Depression to wield a heavy, homemade pushcart through city streets teeming with immigrants. His family's survival depended on his hopes of selling fresh fruit. The father left for market in the early morning and did not return until late evening. The child did not understand that survival created a rift between them. The child felt only a barrier separating them, invisible, authoritative, repressive and silent, all at once.

The father, worn out from his labors, died suddenly at age 50. The scope of dealing with his unexpected death left the child breathless, unable to focus.

The child grew into an adult with a childlike sense of longing for something lost, words of love, a gentle, nurturing touch. Love remained a secret.

The Adult Creator, seeking relief, took crayons in hand, and silently drew out an inner vision of grief. Words were rolling in the adult's mind, like waves cast upon the shore. See King. Seeking. Seeking the Silent Stranger came into focus. Words that had no meaning now inspired an image. Yes, the father had been the king of the child's world.

An explosion of colors vividly appeared to form an image of a blind king crawling out of the sea. One hand raised in greeting. The King of the Sea... Sea King. See King. Seeking. His crowned head encased within a bubble of silence. All the words that could have been said, all the feelings that could have been expressed locked inside the bubble. All the love that could have poured forth encapsulated in a giant tear. It was drowning him as his raised hand reached out.

163

The father had been the primal force in shaping the child's feelings and the adult's thoughts. Yet, like the inner-critic, the father had been of two minds. One was the inhibitor of expression in the child. The other was the giver of permission to be the Adult Creator.

New feelings were added to the picture: helplessness, the inability to change something, the sense that it was too late, the remorse for words unspoken.

The moment of inspiration expressed through a creative act led the Adult Creator to a realization: the Silent Stranger understands death because it gives life to creativity.

—Hyacinthe Kuller Baron, Master Artist,
upon the death of her father
(Illustration #28)

Seeking the Sea King
(Illustration #28)

GLOSSARY

ACCENT: an embellishment used to define a work.

ACCESS: a path or means of approach.

ADULT: an individual who has internalized society's mores.

ADULT CREATOR: the Silent Stranger's role in the creative process.

AREA: the areas of the paper with tonal variations.

ARTIST: anyone who does a creative act.

AUTONOMY: the state of being independent.

BLACK: the area where you impress dark charcoal.

BLEND: smearing the charcoal with pressure on the fingertips.

CHARCOAL: a compressed black stick, round or square, soft or hard, made of charred wood or other organic matter.

COMMIT: to bind to a plan of action.

CONCEPT: an idea.

CONFRONT: to face boldly; a method of acknowledging your inner-critic.

CREATIVITY: artistic or intellectual inventiveness.

CREATOR: a person with artistic or intellectual inventiveness.

DARKS: areas of dark charcoal that create tonal variation.

DARK SHAPES: areas of dark charocal that create the suggestion of a form or shape.

DEFINE: to describe with thick-thin lines.

DEFY: the act of resisting or repudiating the inner-critic.

DEPTH: an illusion created by tones from gray to black.

DIMENSION: an illusion that adds depth to a drawing; executed by tonal variations.

DIRTY: to be covered with residue of charcoal (washable and impermanent).

DISCONCERT: to upset, defeat the inner-critic.

DRAG: pressing down on the charcoal and pushing it around the paper.

DRAWING: the act of representing something on a surface by means of shades and lines.

DYNAMIC: a stroke made with intensity and clarity of purpose.

EMBARRASSMENT: the subjective state of being shamed due to the perception of inappropriate or childish behavior.

ERASE: the use of a kneaded eraser to remove darks, imply shape, provide movement.

FAITH: the capacity to experience self-trust in order to express innate creativity.

FACILITATE: to create an easy access for the mental pathway to the Silent Stranger.

FEELINGS: the motivating impetus behind the strokes you make with your fingers.

FUNCTIONAL: mentally capable and sound.

HYPOTHESIS: an unproven theory.

IMAGE: the appearance of a recognizable likeness that appears without volition.

IMAGINATION: the act or power of creating mental images from the marks you make.

IMPEDIMENT: a physical or mental block or barrier.

IMPULSIVE: making marks and strokes without thinking, only feeling.

INDIVIDUALITY: the sum total of characteristics that make a person unique.

INNER CHILD: a pop-psychology concept based on the concept of injury to the psyche during childhood causing a block to self-fulfillment as an adult.

INNER-CRITIC: the ego-protective, negative aspect of the inner dialogue.

INNER DIALOGUE: the subliminal voice that monitors your inner reality.

INNER SELF: your internal (mental) reality.

INNER VISION: images formed from your inner-reality which are consciously appreciated.

INNER-VOICE: the positive, ego protective aspect of the inner dialogue.

KNEADING: the act of pulling and shaping the moldable eraser.

LIGHT AREAS: sections where the white paper shows through your applied marks.

MORES: folkways; rules that are conducive to the good of society.

NUANCE: a finite degree of difference perceivable by the senses.

OBJECTIVE: an analytical perspective versus a subjective perspective.

PATHWAY: the mental access (road) to your Silent Stranger.

PERMISSION: allowing yourself to make marks without a predefined format.

PRESS: to apply pressure to the charcoal or to your charcoal soiled fingertips.

PROCEDURES: the sequence in which materials or skills are utilized.

PULL: forcing the eraser through the marks to define, create highlights or a sense of movement.

RANDOM: to apply without a predefined plan.

REALITY: may be overt (apparent to others); or covert (see INNER SELF).

REGRESSION: the return to earlier behavior patterns.

REPETITION: to perform more than once in order to reinforce a skill.

REPRESSION: the act of suppressing consciously painful acts, impulses and ideas to a subconcious level.

RESEMBLE: alternative images you recognize in your charcoal smears.

RESIDUE: the powder remaining when the charcoal breaks up.

RUB: the act of repetitively applying the charocal and blending with the fingers.

SEE: the capacity to perceive from a new or intuitive perspective.

SELF DISCOVERY: the breakthrough that clarifies your motivations.

SIGNING: acknowledging your work by artistically putting your signature to it.

SILENT STRANGER: the creative aspect of your psyche that occurs after melding the rational adult with your renewed child-like capacity for visual imagery.

SMEAR, SMEARS: the random brushing of the fingers, hands, and the dirty eraser.

SOCIALIZATION: the process of absorbing society's rules or folkways.

SOCIETY: the social structure in which you live.

SOCIOPATH: an amoral individual who has not developed a conscience. According to Freudian dynamics, an individual who has not internalized a superego (has not internalized society's mores).

SPONTANEOUS: performing an act without forethought.

SQUINT: narrowing the eyelids to focus on a small portion or area.

STROKE, STROKING: the act of blending the charcoal with the fingers. See RUB above.

SUBJECTIVE: from an introspective point of view.

SUBLIMATING INVECTIVE: a positive admonition that blocks negative thoughts.

SWIPE: a stroke with a staccato (abrupt) quality to its application.

TRAITS: characteristics.

TRUST: the capacity to act on faith.

TRUTH: a provable fact.

WITH ABANDON: with unrestrained freedom.

BIBLIOGRAPHY & SUGGESTED READINGS

Bach, Richard. *Illusions: The Adventures of a Reluctant Messiah.* U.S.A.: Delacorte Press, 1977.

Barron, Frank. *Creativity and Psychological Health: Origins of Personal Vitality and Creative Freedom.* New York: C.E.F. Press, 1990.

Beck, Aaron T., M.D. *Cognitive Therapy and the Emotional Disorders.* New York: New American Library Trade, 1993.

Bradshaw, John. *Homecoming: Reclaiming and Championing Your Inner Child.* New York: Bantam Books, 1990.

Cameron, Julia. *The Artist's Way: A Spiritual Path to Higher Creativity.* New York: G.P. Putnam's Sons, 1992.

Castaneda, Carlos. *A Separate Reality: Further Conversations with Don Juan.* New York: Pocket Books, 1972.

Clance, Pauline Rose. *The Impostor Phenomenon: Overcoming the Fear That Haunts Your Success.* Atlanta: Peachtree Publishers, LTD., 1985.

Edwards, Betty. *Drawing on the Right Side of the Brain: A Course in Enhancing Creativity and Artistic Confidence.* Los Angeles: J. P. Tarcher, Inc., 1989.

Gross, Nancy E. *Living With Stress.* New York: McGraw-Hill, 1958.

Jung, C. G. *The Undiscovered Self.* New York: Little Brown & Company, 1957.

Rhyne, Janie. *The Gestalt Art Experience.* Monterey, CA: Brooks/Cole, 1973.

Samuels, Mike, M.D., et al. *Seeing With The Mind's Eye.* New York: Random House, 1975.

Steinbeck, John. *Sweet Thursday.* New York: Penguin USA, 1996.

INDEX

Lidia E. Everett, M.D.

❀　❀　❀

LIDIA E. EVERETT is a Board Certified Internist. Over and above her concern for her profession, she has been interested in the impact that changing cultural backgrounds and life styles have on individual well-being.

Her interest was stimulated by the exodus of her family from Cuba in the early 60's after Castro's takeover. The cultural impact was significant. Most of her mother's family were professionals and sacrificed extensively in order to revalidate their professional education. Through their example, she was motivated to pave her own way.

She founded and worked in a clinic for impoverished Mexican Indians. She was the first woman and first foreign medical graduate to serve in a position of honor as "Chief Medical Resident" for the University of California at Irvine-Long Beach Veteran's Administration residency program.

While working in private practice at Scripp's Memorial Hospital, Lidia became interested in professional "burn-out" and worked extensively with her peers to diversify their interests. She was a speaker on the topic of burn-out for "Women of the Eighties."

Lidia became an outspoken advocate for her patients during the transition from "fee for service" to HMO medicine in both the press and radio and television talk-shows. She has also scripted and produced vocational rehabilitation films and has been a collaborator in the script for a major motion picture.

Her interests include travel, fishing, scuba diving, equine exhibition, classical piano, and macro-photography.

❀　❀　❀

Hyacinthe Kuller Baron

❃ ❃ ❃

HYACINTHE KULLER BARON is a master artist whose professional career has spanned forty years. Described in numerous publications as a gifted "wild child," she discovered in her mid-twenties that anything was possible if an individual was free to express creativity. This realization led to the motivating factor of her artistic existence: to awaken individuals to their aesthetic appreciation.

In the early 1970's Hyacinthe explored the role of woman as artist, business person and nurturer by executing editions of lithographs on the themes of Motherhood, Childhood, and Sisterhood. Many of them found their way into private and public collections as well as the Smithsonian.

Hyacinthe was the first woman to have an art gallery on New York's Madison Avenue, the first of many galleries she has maintained with her husband of twenty-seven years. Celebrity collectors and devoted clientele were the inspiration for Hyacinthe to try her talents at designing award-winning fashions. Her designs led to successful business opportunities and avenues of expression and recognition.

Hyacinthe was inspired by her private art students to refine her *Making Your Mark*™ Technique and Exercises. She strove to empower adults to easily access their own creativity.

As Chair of the *Making Your Mark*™ Workshops and Artist in Residence at the San Diego Center for the Blind, she proved that inner vision is a key to self-expression, and introduced handicapped individuals to the rewards of achieving self-fulfillment through art.

Hyacinthe is currently writing a book about her extraordinary experiences in life and art. A published poet and produced playwright, she is polishing up a mythological trilogy inspired by her paintings and sculptures. In addition, she is at work on a screenplay and several series of paintings inspired by her esoteric philosophies.

Hyacinthe enjoys life aboard a boat, reflecting on the amazing odyssey she and her husband have shared. The reward of being an artist is the freedom to be available when adventure or inspiration occur—and the joy of being a playful, if no longer, wild child.

❃ ❃ ❃

COMMUNE-A-KEY PUBLISHING
AND SEMINARS

Commune-A-Key Publishing and Seminars was established in 1992. Our mission statement, "Communicating Keys to Growth and Empowerment," describes our effort to publish books that inspire and promote personal growth and wellness. Our books and products provide powerful ways to care for, discover and heal ourselves and others.

Our audience includes health care professionals and counselors, caregivers, men, women, people interested in Native American traditions—anyone interested in personal growth, psychology, and inspiration. We hope you enjoy this book! If you have any comments, questions, or would like to be on our mailing list for future products and seminars, please write or call us at the address and phone number below.

ORDERING INFORMATION

Commune-A-Key Publishing has a variety of books and products. For further information on our books and audio tapes, or if you would like to receive a catalog, please write or call us at the address and phone number listed below.

Our authors are also available for seminars, workshops and lectures. Please call our toll-free number for further information.

COMMUNE-A-KEY PUBLISHING

P.O. Box 58637
Salt Lake City, UT 84158

❀

1-800-983-0600